William Brash Macleod

The Afflictions of the Righteous as Discussed in the Book of Job and in the Light of the Gospel

William Brash Macleod

The Afflictions of the Righteous as Discussed in the Book of Job and in the Light of the Gospel

ISBN/EAN: 9783337253394

Printed in Europe, USA, Canada, Australia, Japan

Cover: Foto ©Lupo / pixelio.de

More available books at **www.hansebooks.com**

THE AFFLICTIONS OF THE RIGHTEOUS

AS DISCUSSED IN THE BOOK OF JOB AND

IN THE NEW LIGHT OF THE GOSPEL

BY

W. B. MACLEOD

MINISTER OF THE CANDLISH UNITED FREE CHURCH
EDINBURGH

"Many are the afflictions of the righteous;
But the Lord delivereth him out of them all"
PSALM xxxiv. 19

HODDER AND STOUGHTON
LONDON   NEW YORK   TORONTO

To my Friend
HUGH BLACK,
whose Friendship
has been,
and is,
an Inspiration

PREFACE

NOTWITHSTANDING its great antiquity the book of Job is probably the most intensely modern of all the books in the Bible. Among others, which need not be named, this is one chief reason why it deserves the special attention of the present generation.

Many books have been written on this great book; but of course that is no reason why it should not be made the subject of a fresh course of study. Each successive generation of men will claim the privilege and exercise the right of studying anew these sacred writings which constitute the Bible in the light of such new knowledge and opportunity as may come to them in the progressive providence of God.

So far as I am aware the present work endeavours to conduct the study of this ancient book along lines which have never been followed by any previous writer on the subject. Hitherto it has been the usual practice to examine each speech in detail in the order in which they occur, a method which is admirably adapted to the minute exegetical study of the text, but which has several obvious disadvantages when the object in view is to obtain a comprehensive grasp of the great questions discussed, and to make a just and true estimate of the comparative value of the opposing arguments as a whole.

Now the chief feature in the new method which is introduced in the following pages consists in this, that while due consideration is given to the individual characteristics of each speaker, and to the original elements which he contributes to the debate, and while the difference between Job's method of arguing with his friends and his remarkable way of expostulating with God concerning the same high themes is brought into clear relief by separate treatment, yet the different groups of arguments which represent the different positions discussed with reference to the problems of human suffering and the moral government of the world are each focussed into a unity, and finally condensed into a series of propositions.

Further, in this twentieth century of the Christian era, it is, I believe, a grave error to discuss the great problems with which this book of Job is concerned as if they ought to be still as perplex-

PREFACE

ing to us as they were to Job, and as if Christ had not come and brought life and immortality to light. Therefore, throughout the successive chapters of the present work, an earnest effort is made to show the supreme worth of the Christian interpretation of those otherwise inexplicable problems —an intrepretation which really, according to the promise, "turneth the shadow of death into the morning."

I venture to entertain the hope that this new method of treating this remarkable and confessedly difficult book will be found to possess some important advantages, and in particular that it may be useful to some readers in helping them to bring the great questions with which the debate is concerned more clearly to an issue before their own minds.

W. B. MACLEOD.

CANDLISH MANSE,
    EDINBURGH.

CONTENTS

CHAPTER I

THE BOOK AND ITS PROBLEM

Preliminary difficulties—Authorship—Date—Historicity—Structure of the Book—Its central problem—Its supernatural element—Its conception of God—Its doctrine of Satan—The character of Job 1–21

CHAPTER II

TRIAL BY SUFFERING LOVE

The two stages of Job's trial—Initial problem of destruction of life and property—Poetic idealism of the Book—Moral significance of material loss to Job—Contrast between bereavement in Job's day and bereavement to the Christian—Job's behaviour under trial—Bereavement as discipline—As the test of faith—The praise of sorrow 22–42

CHAPTER III

TRIAL BY PHYSICAL PAIN

The second scene in heaven—Job's "Integrity"—The two divine ends in Job's suffering—Satan's new insinuation against Job—His new challenge to God—The divine restriction of Satan's power—The problem of pain—Job's extreme case—Its bearing on traditional doctrine—Modern interest of the problem—The function of human pain 43–63

CHAPTER IV

JOB'S WIFE AND FRIENDS

Character of Job's wife—Why her attitude differs from that of the friends—Why Job's attitude differs from that of both his wife and friends—Characteristics of the three friends—Their similarity and individuality—Their virtues and faults—Their function in the debate—Whitewashing God's providence—Mystery and presumption—The Christian explanation 64–85

CHAPTER V

JOB'S LAMENT OF LIFE

Job's failure and its cause—The silent behaviour of the friends—Need of just discrimination—Sympathy and accusation—The tragic passion of Job's lament—The faults of his pessimism—False optimism and true—Job's contempt of suicide—The new light on Job's dark problem 86–106

CHAPTER VI

THE ORTHODOX ARGUMENT AGAINST JOB

The arguments of the friends compared and contrasted—Elements of sameness and repetition—Elements of individual originality—The arguments considered as a unity and condensed into six propositions—Criticism of the argument—Its high aim and points of strength and beauty—Its cruelty towards Job—Its false championship of God 107–142

CONTENTS xiii

CHAPTER VII

JOB'S REPLY TO HIS FRIENDS

PAGES

The heterodoxy of Job—His complaint of injustice—His defence of himself—His reply to the argument from God's greatness—His problem of personal justification—The crux of the debate—The justification of God—Job's "Sanctuaries of darkness"—Characteristics of his darkest moods—The quality of his faith—The crisis of the whole book—The difficulty of Job's last speech—Condensation of Job's argument . . . 143-179

CHAPTER VIII

JOB'S EXPOSTULATIONS WITH GOD

Job's appeal from men to God—His complaint against God—Its amazing boldness—Its frank honesty—The responsibilities of the Creator in relation to His creatures—The master minds of literature and Job's problem—Superiority of Job's treatment of it—The grounds of Job's prayers for death—The silence of God—Contrast between Old Testament and New Testament saints in suffering—Job's expostulations with God in regard to his own sin—His questions answered in Christ . 180-207

CHAPTER IX

THE INTERVENTION OF ELIHU

Characteristics of Elihu—The purpose of his intervention—The integrity of the book discussed—Elihu's method of argument—His criticism of Job's argument—His appeal to the "Wise men"—His attack on Job's character—His answer to Job's complaints—His original contribution to the discussion—Criticism of Elihu's speech 208-241

CHAPTER X

THE DIVINE INTERPRETATION

The great speech of Jehovah—Its supreme poetic power—Impressiveness of its argument—Its central purpose—Its combination of majesty and gentleness—A series of impressive contrasts—Significance of Job's response to the divine challenge—Job's silence not enough for God—What Job's criticism of God's providence involved—The divine self-revelation and its end—Job's unreserved confession—The undeniable incompleteness of Jehovah's speech—Its remarkable omissions—What it leaves to be added by Christ 242-274

CHAPTER XI

THE EPILOGUE

The great value of the epilogue—Grounds of the divine anger against the three friends—Job made priest and intercessor for his critics—His intercession the opening of the gates of his captivity—" Poetic justice "—The ideality of Job's rewards—Summary of the principal teachings of the book 275-297

CHAPTER I

THE BOOK AND ITS PROBLEM

IN entering upon a series of studies in the book of Job I am very sensible of the difficulty of the task which I thus attempt to undertake. But the great central questions which are discussed with such amazing penetration and power in this book are full of an ever-fresh and commanding interest to every earnest mind; and we can never gain anything, but on the contrary must lose much, by turning aside and neglecting such questions on the ground that they are deep and difficult. Life is difficult, although we are constantly trying in unworthy ways to make it easy; and life is deep, however we may do our poor best to make it shallow enough. And the great questions with which this book is concerned are among the deepest and most real we know, because they deal with man's relation to God, and with God's relation to man, in connection with that mystery of human pain which is ever with us, and which at times presses upon all human hearts with a terrible weight, and even strains the faith of religious men to the very uttermost.

I am therefore hopeful that the difficulties of dealing with this book in such a series of studies may be so far overcome as to amply reward us for our search after the truth by a clearer apprehension of these great principles of God's Providence which it discusses, and by the acquisition of some profound practical lessons, which may well be of the greatest service to us in the most critical seasons and the most trying experiences of life.

The manner in which I propose to conduct these studies may be briefly stated thus :—I will endeavour, on the one hand, to get at and to set forth the original meaning of the teaching, in relation to the men who occupied the actual historical situation of those to whom it was first addressed. And, on the other hand, I will steadily endeavour to show how deep a meaning many parts of that ancient teaching have for us to-day, and how clearly that teaching reveals to us the immensity of our debt to the fuller, fairer light that has come to us through Jesus Christ our Lord. In this opening study I will make some introductory remarks concerning some more or less important

THE BOOK AND ITS PROBLEM 3

preliminary questions, and consider broadly the central problem of the book, and the characteristics of the three principal figures, God, Satan, and Job, as presented here.

First, a word about authorship. Very little need be said of this, for the minimum of information required to make a discussion on this point either useful or effective simply does not exist. Some have suggested that the book was written by Moses; and others that its author was Job himself. Lightfoot thinks that it might have been written by Elihu, the fifth speaker in the debate. Some of our best Biblical scholars, such as Delitzsch and Godet, think it very probable that it was written by one of the wise men of Solomon's brilliant court, and Godet suggests Heman, the author of the eighty-eighth psalm.

But the simple truth is that we have no reliable information as to who wrote the book; and I like well the remark of Dr A. B. Davidson in this connection. He says:—" There are some minds that cannot put up with uncertainty and are under the necessity of deluding themselves into quietude by fixing some known name. There are others to whom it is a comfort to think that in this omniscient age a few things still remain mysterious."

4 AFFLICTIONS OF THE RIGHTEOUS

The fact is that we know just as little about who wrote the book of Job as we do about who wrote the Epistle to the Hebrews; and yet there are no parts of the Bible whose high function in the organic unity of God's revelation to men, from intrinsic evidence, will less bear to be questioned than these.

Then much has also been written about the date of this book; but it will be well to say even less here about the date than has been said about the authorship. Widely differing scholars have filled up the whole period between Moses and the end of the Babylonian captivity with their unwearied speculations. Godet argues with considerable plausibility, that its date might be the golden age of Solomon. Davidson says that it was written not earlier than the seventh century B.C.; and Dr Watson that it was produced between the first and second of the Isaian oracles. But it would be unprofitable to enter into any exhaustive discussion of this question here. Professor Peake thinks that the date might perhaps be near the close of the fifth century B.C.; but every serious student of the book will agree with him when he adds—" while it may take some of its colour from the dark experiences of its time it really

THE BOOK AND ITS PROBLEM 5

contributes little to our understanding of it to connect it closely with any set of historical conditions." In any case it is quite clear that the story itself refers to a much earlier time than the earliest date that can reasonably be suggested for the authorship of the book.

The next preliminary question is much more important. It is whether the story is history or allegory. About this, too, there has been much discussion, and on this point we have reasonable grounds for having something more definite to say than we had in connection with the two preceding points. The real answer seems to be that it is neither history, as we understand history, nor is it mere allegory alone, but it is partly both. The opening scene in heaven, the free use of the symbolical numbers three and seven in describing Job's flocks and children, the dramatic and ideal account of Job's calamities, and especially the highly wrought poetic and philosophical discussion, show beyond all reasonable doubt that the book is not intended to be ordinary history as we now understand it. On the other hand it is impossible to doubt that Job was a real person without doing violence both to the text of the book itself, and also to the testimony of other Bible authors. The book opens with the words—" There dwelt a man in the land of Uz, whose name was Job ; and that man was perfect and upright, and one that feared God, and eschewed evil." Ezekiel speaks of Job together with Enoch and Noah, and he has no more doubt of the historical personality of the one than he has of the others. The reference of James in the new Testament is to the same effect. The idea that Job represents the Jewish Church is so purely fanciful as not to merit serious notice. Luther, as he very often did, strikes the golden mean here also when he says—" I hold the book of Job to be a record of facts ; but that everything happened just as it is recorded I do not believe."

The truth seems to be that we have here a series of well-known facts in a certain life story divinely used by an inspired prophet as the basis of some of the greatest lessons which were ever taught to mankind. And the fact that everything did not happen just as it is recorded in no way affects the worth or divine authority of the work as an instrument of spiritual education. This is attested by Ezekiel, by Paul, by Peter, and by James ; but most of all this is assured by the internal evidence of the work. Carlyle well says in his " Heroes and Hero Worship "—" I call the book

THE BOOK AND ITS PROBLEM 7

of Job one of the greatest things ever written with pen. There is nothing written in the Bible or out of it of equal literary merit." Froude, also a very high authority on such a question, calls it— " A book which will one day perhaps, when it is allowed to stand on its own merits, be seen towering up alone, far above all the poetry of the world." Such a book well merits the earnest study of all intelligent minds, not only as standing at the head of the world's literature, but as being an invaluable guide to all seekers after truth.

As to the structure of the book it is a dramatic poem. The prose prologue occupies the first two chapters. This introduces the highly poetic discussion which is carried on by Job on the one side and by his friends, Eliphaz, Bildad, and Zophar on the other, who each reply alternately to the arguments of Job. This goes on till the close of the thirty-first chapter. There is then a short prose passage consisting of the first five verses of the thirty-second chapter, introducing the prolonged speech of the young man Elihu, who criticises both Job on the one hand, and his three friends on the other hand, and to whom they all four listen without interruption.

This young speaker prophetically intimates that

8 AFFLICTIONS OF THE RIGHTEOUS

God will answer for Himself. And so, in the thirty-eighth chapter, in which God Himself answers Job out of the whirlwind, the wonderful majesty both of thought and expression exhibited in the book reach a climax which is almost oppressive in its amazing power and beauty. This is immediately followed by Job's humble confession of his own sin and foolish presumption. Then the last eleven verses of the book form the brief prose epilogue, in which Job is ideally blessed, and becomes also the divinely appointed priest to intercede for his three erring friends.

Readers of Browning's "Rabbi Ben Ezra," "A Death in the Desert," and "Easter Day," are forcibly reminded of the Book of Job; but it is only to see with what a lonely majesty the author of this book towers above even so great a genius as that of Robert Browning. Whatever we may not be able to say as to the date, or the authorship, or the historicity of this book, we are able to say this of it at least, and to say it with an untroubled confidence, that if there be any writing in all the world which is in the truest sense inspired of God this book of Job most certainly is.

What, then, is the central problem of the book? Briefly, it is to reconcile the justice of an almighty

THE BOOK AND ITS PROBLEM 9

and good God with the actual sufferings, not of bad men, nor even with the sufferings of the human race in general, but with the actual sufferings of good men in this world. It is impossible for us to suppose that God tortures good men as some men torture inferior animals, for what they call their amusement or sport. And we must observe that there is no hint of vicarious suffering in the book, such as we have in the later prophecies of Isaiah and subsequent Hebrew prophets, and the meaning of which is fully unfolded to us in the experience of Jesus Christ. That is not the question which is discussed in this book at all. It is a wholly different question, namely: Why do good men suffer, as we see they do suffer, under the reign of omnipotent goodness? This is surely a question of intensest interest and of deepest importance to every son of man and every daughter of woman to-day.

We must observe at the outset that the key to the whole book is to be found in Satan's question— " Doth Job fear God for naught ? " and in the combined answer of God and of Job to that question. For we must note that this is not a question which God can answer fully alone. He needs the co-operation of His servant to answer it; and He also needs the co-operation of His servant undergoing the experience of mysterious suffering to answer it conclusively. Hence the book is absolutely opposed to all sordid materialism. It shows that the deepest roots of man's life are in the unseen : that a good man's life is most closely, and even inseparably related to the invisible God. Surely this also is a truth for to-day.

This book shows, even as Christ's parables show, that there is a power of goodness and a power of evil that strive concerning man's life ; and that the human will is free, and is the umpire for itself, and for its own fate, whether for goodness and against evil, or for evil and against goodness. These facts are concentrated for us in the question of Satan—" Doth Job fear God for naught ? " Observe that it is not enough that a man serve God, nor even that he serve Him freely. It is required also, and not merely by any arbitrary divine command but by the highest laws of a man's own life and well-being, that he serve God unselfishly, that is, from love of God Himself, and from love of His service for its own sake.

Any other kind of service, whatever superficial and transient gain it might bring to the creature, could certainly bring no glory to the Creator.

THE BOOK AND ITS PROBLEM 11

This is the very point of Satan's challenge. This also is why God accepts the challenge. This is why Job is called to suffering, and such suffering. It is that his suffering in the true spirit of God's servant, amid the most fearful perplexity as to the cause of his suffering, so utterly misconceived and misrepresented by his friends, should be the demonstration of his love for God, and of his faith in God.

Now what are the chief characteristics of the three central figures, God, Job, and Satan, as presented to us in this book? In the first place God is conceived as of the One absolutely omnipotent Sovereign. This characteristic of the divine Being appears again and again, and in every part of the book; in the prologue, in the speeches of Job and of his opponents alike, in the great speech of God most of all, and even in the brief epilogue, where God finally apportions the praise and the blame. The names by which God is called throughout the book also emphasise the idea. He is Eloah, the Lofty One; Shaddai, the Almighty One; Jehovah, the Lord.

But in the book God is not only the absolute Sovereign; He is also absolutely just, and He is so notwithstanding all appearances to the contrary.

In the prologue Satan's power over Job is strictly limited, not only because God is Sovereign, but because He is a just Sovereign; and therefore there is already a hint of the happy end in the evil beginning. But because of appearances there is need of humble faith and patience. This is still the situation in our own time. As the New Testament expresses it—" Without faith it is impossible to please Him." There are still present with us the mysterious, inexplicable facts which raise strange questionings and give opportunity to the play of testing doubts and fears; and from these there is no refuge save in the exercise of a reasonable faith which rests itself upon the character of God, and believes, notwithstanding all appearances to the contrary, that He is just.

But further, the God of this book is a supremely benevolent Being. He takes pleasure in His good creature, because he is good, and makes His boast of him, and ever behind all the machinations of Satan, works for his good. And yet, observe, God's wish for Job's good is more evidently set forth than His work for that end in the book. The author has no such glorious idea as that in the New Testament—God as incarnate love serving His creatures for His creatures' good. This was a

THE BOOK AND ITS PROBLEM 13

further revelation of the divine nature which was reserved for the work of His Son.

The last characteristic of God revealed in this book is mystery. He is the hidden God. His ways and His wisdom are inscrutable. Man cannot judge Him, but can only wait upon Him with becoming humility; for the mind of man is so far below the mind of God that his only wisdom is to recognise that his times are in God's hand, and to bow before Him as his Maker and ultimate Vindicator in reverent and adoring awe. This also is a lesson that is profoundly needed in this present time, when impatient boldness and irreverence are so prominent in the thoughts and in the conduct of men, and even of children.

But this revelation also has been richly supplemented by the Son of God, who has shown us God's inmost heart as One who not only subjects the creature He loves to suffering, but in His own self-abnegating love suffers Himself, even unto death, for His creature's sake. God's ways are still in many respects inscrutable to us, because He so immeasurably transcends us; but now we are sure of His heart. We know that: we can never doubt that again, for Christ has fully revealed it. However deep life's trials may be, and however

14 AFFLICTIONS OF THE RIGHTEOUS

dark may sometimes be the way in which we are compelled to go, and however terrible may be the spectres of the mind that such experiences raise, we can now always fall back upon the great unanswerable challenge of Paul—" He that spared not His own Son but gave Him up for us all, how shall He not with Him also freely give us all things ? "

The character of Satan also in this book, though it is an imperfect sketch, is nevertheless in perfect harmony with all the later teaching of the Bible on the subject. A distinguished theologian has pointed out the striking fact that the Bible teaching is in contrast with the teaching of all other religions in this respect, that while in all other religions the tendency is to diffuse the personality of the central principle of evil into more and more vague forms of thought as time goes on, the Bible theology tends to focus the power of evil more and more in an intense personality.

Now it is most noteworthy that in this respect the greatest authors have followed the Bible. There are several great conceptions of Satan outside the Bible, and to contrast and compare these with the Bible conception would be a study of very

THE BOOK AND ITS PROBLEM 15

great interest. Dante's Satan is a grotesquely horrible and gigantic monster, with three faces, six eyes, and "tears of bloody foam." Bunyan's Diabolus hovers between the conception of Dante and that of Robert Burns. In Bunyan Satan is always a cunning, cruel, and relentless being, of whom he always thinks very grimly. Burns, on the other hand, habitually considered Satan a fit subject for humour, and he could hardly ever write of him without a touch of pity. Very different again from these conceptions of Satan is Goethe's Mephistopheles, whose chief characteristic is a pitiless, cynical gaiety. He is a laughing devil who enjoys himslf immensely in working the ruin of man. Milton's Satan, again, is a most regal being, the emperor of a mighty kingdom, the god of Pandemonium and supreme in his own sphere. But, in strong contrast to Goethe's Mephistopheles, he is a most solemn and mournful devil, with no gleam of joy in his life, a being who says—" Which way I fly is hell, myself am hell, and in the lowest deep a lower deep still threatening to devour me opens wide."

Now the Satan of the book of Job is neither grotesque, nor gay, nor regal, nor horribly repulsive in shape. But he is such a being as to present no points of attraction for our admiration, or our sympathy, or our pity. He is a creature whose character is altogether contemptible and abhorrent to every good and just soul. This is how the Bible always presents Satan. He is never described except symbolically. His special characteristic is to do, and to lead others to do, evil. But he is still the slave of God, and is never presented as an antagonist on equal terms with Him. He can do nothing without divine permission. He tempts and troubles God's saints on sufferance, and only for a season. He is bound and loosed, and finally cast into the lake of fire, according to the ordination of Him who is sovereign everywhere, and who "worketh all things according to the counsel of His own will." Nay, in working the ruin of man the Bible Satan is ever subject to the will of man as well as to the will of God, for man himself is represented as being "invincible upon the field, he cannot fall unless he yield."

Now Satan is specially realised by each soul in that pressure to cherish evil thought, and to do evil, which he experiences in the direction of his besetting sin. Where a man's nature and circumstances conspire to make him weakest, there—as even in the case of the temptation of Jesus in the

THE BOOK AND ITS PROBLEM 17

wilderness—the attack of the evil power is concentrated, and God permits this for most Godlike ends. Thus we find that our individual experience of Satan is in perfect harmony with the Bible teaching concerning him.

Let us now look at Job, the third principal figure in the book. The first notable thing about him is his nationality. Very significant is the fact that he is not a Jew but an Arab. He is a man of Uz, and the scene of his trial is an oasis in the Arabian desert. Here we have a most striking example of how God can reach the heathen world, and of the truth of the great confession of Peter, which, however, even he only learned to make with great difficulty. " Of a truth I perceive that God is no respecter of persons, but in every nation he that feareth Him and worketh righteousness is accepted of Him."

The author of Job is the fore-runner of that glorious Petrine as well as Pauline universalism which means a Gospel for the world. Many modern Christians have not made this great truth entirely their own even yet. They know that Jesus Christ is the one Saviour of men; but they are still tempted to give way to the strange presumption of daring to limit the operation of God's

18 AFFLICTIONS OF THE RIGHTEOUS

Spirit in bringing righteous souls consciously under the beams of that great Light that lighteth every man that cometh into the world. Can we not see that God is able to reveal Himself to a righteous Buddhist or Mohammedan to-day as He did of old to the heathen Arab, Job, and to many other righteous souls who sought Him in the darkness before Christ's name was known? Consider what is said of Job's character. " That man was perfect and upright." It is an ethical test.

In his great trial Job certainly shows some self-righteousness, and much temper, and no little irreverence towards God; and for these things God reproves him as well as his friends. Yet, because Job steadily struggled towards perfection, God called him a perfect and upright man. Thus we see that what we sincerely long to be, and labour to be, is even more important than what we are. This is so because, if only we remain faithful to it, our ideal will certainly one day be realised. This is a most important principle. It is what justifies the strange song of Robert Browning—

" What I desired to be,
And was not, comforts me."

Now consider Job's circumstances. His wealth is reckoned in eastern and patriarchal fashion,

THE BOOK AND ITS PROBLEM 19

but it is very great in reference to the time. He has also seven sons and three daughters; and we are shown by a skilful touch how he is the true high-priest of his family. The picture has no shadow. It is one of almost perfect earthly happiness. Observe the relation of all this to the great moral problem which is to be discussed. It was the fixed orthodox belief in that old time that prosperity was the special mark of divine favour. Therefore it was the special temptation of Job to fall into a state of self-satisfaction and self-righteousness.

Now the challenge of Satan is directly in this line—" Doth Job fear God for naught ? " The sneer has force. It pays Job to be religious. Satan insinuates that Job's is merely a commercial religion. This false doctrine that sin and suffering, and righteousness and prosperity, are flexible equations runs through the whole history of the Old Testament from Genesis to Malachi. Men held this false doctrine as a first principle, and then, because the facts of life could not be squared with it, they grumbled and revolted against God, asking as even Malachi has to report—" It is vain to serve God; and what profit is it that we have kept His charge, and that we have walked mournfully before the Lord of Hosts ? " Is not this the very attitude which many still adopt towards the service of God, though they may express it in somewhat different ways ?

This whole situation, then, has a most modern interest and importance. God does not only ask a man whether he is religious, but why ? Is it for selfish gain ? Is it for the help and credit it yields him now, or even for the sake of the good things he hopes for in heaven ? This is the evil side of other-worldliness. This book of Job is the first great attack on this false doctrine on which so many superficially religious lives have been based ; and how it tests religious motives. The deepest doctrine in this book is that man to be truly saved must love goodness and truth for their own sakes, and God for what He is and not for what He gives. This means character. And there is no salvation apart from character.

Consider the unspeakable difference between loving God because He is altogether lovely and loveable to us, and simulating a love for Him for the sake of what we may get from Him. Think of the whole heaven that lies between serving God for any external reward merely and serving Him because we find that serving Him is its own supreme

THE BOOK AND ITS PROBLEM

reward! In this way we may see that this old challenge of Satan has many things to teach us yet, and has a far closer contact with our modern life and its problems than we may have been disposed to think. For if there was need that God should test Abraham and Job are we so sure that there is no need that He should test us? Shall we not rather ask with Robert Browning—

> "Is not God now i' the world His power first made?
> Is not His love at issue still with sin,
> Visibly when a wrong is done on earth?
> Love, wrong, and pain, what see I else around?
> Yea, and the resurrection and uprise
> To the right hand of the throne.—What is it beside
> When such truth, breaking bounds, o'erfloods my soul,
> And, as I saw the sin and death, even so
> See I the need yet transiency of both,
> The good and glory consummated thence?"

CHAPTER II

TRIAL BY SUFFERING LOVE

WE have already seen that this great book is idealised history, and that its central purpose is to reconcile in human reason, so far as that is possible to our limited knowledge and understanding, the sovereign rule of an almighty and good God with the sufferings of the good. In discussing the poetic machinery by which the author proceeds to the accomplishment of his purpose we saw that in the preliminary scene in heaven it was decided by God, in answer to Satan's base insinuation, to subject Job to severe, although limited trial, for the revelation of the divine glory in the perfecting of Job's faith. This strange celestial scene is now succeeded by the opening scene on earth, in which the saint actually passes through the first stage of his awful ordeal. It is chiefly trial by suffering love ; but to this is prefixed with a Satanic ingenuity trial by worldly loss on such a scale as alone might well shake deeply even a

TRIAL BY SUFFERING LOVE 23

good man's faith, and which certainly accentuates to the uttermost the far more terrible part of this first testing which immediately succeeds it.

Satan is represented as being in an eager haste to go as far as he has power to go in the troubling of God's beloved; for to forget that Job, through all his sufferings, *is* God's beloved would be to miss the main point in the book. The trial of Job is divided into two clearly marked stages. In the first of these Satan strikes at the faith and religious devotion of Job through what is his—that is, by the utter ruin of all his material possessions, and by the death of all his beloved children. In the second stage of the trial, Satan, having obtained larger liberty in his evil work, again attempts the same thing by severest personal affliction through physical pain, and in the course of this second trial, added to all that has gone before, he heaps upon the devoted servant of God every description of misery which a man may endure while yet there remains to him a bare and wretched existence, from which he longs to be free.

We have to consider the first of these stages of trial now. But there is an important preliminary question which will occur to almost every thoughtful reader of the prologue of this remarkable book, namely, what view are we to take of the general wreck, not merely of property, but also of human and animal life which is involved in the first stage of this divinely permitted trial of Job ? For on a superficial reading all these things seem to happen merely in order that Job may be tried. To many minds this may present a difficulty which I would not willingly ignore

Now a large part of the answer to this difficulty lies in the designed ideality of the narrative, which I have already discussed. Every earnest student of this book will, like Martin Luther, perceive the conclusive evidence of this idealising element in many things—as for example in the sudden massing together of Job's calamities, the messengers coming in after each other like well-regulated clock-work, just at the last sentence of the one that precedes, thus reporting the successive disasters with cumulative and crushing effect. Or again, the same thing is observable in the manner in which each at the close of his melancholy tidings repeats the same words—" And I only am escaped alone to tell thee," like a constantly recurring refrain in some deeply tragic song. These things, and such as these, show us plainly that we are here not in the region of plain prose history, but are dealing with facts

TRIAL BY SUFFERING LOVE 25

which have been poetically touched by the suggestive genius of a great spiritual teacher, who often abridges, conceals, and colours, that he may the more skilfully entice the soul of his readers to the exercise of intense reflection and the discovery of deeper spiritual truth. What is suggested to us by what is not told, and what priceless treasures we gather from the ideal glow with which the bald facts are often illuminated as with a radiant light from heaven—these things are hardly less wonderful than what we have explicitly set forth in those majestic combinations of words which make their appeal not to the reason alone. The inspired poet clearly felt when he wrote this remarkable prologue that sudden death, even in the case of man, was by no means the most mysterious of God's providences, and this, too, let us remember, without the rising of that glorious Sun of righteousness which brought life and immortality to light.

There was also, doubtless, present to such a mind as his the fact that in all such destruction of human life as he here records every life so suddenly ended is alway co-related in countless subtle and mysterious ways to many other lives and not to one alone; even as, for example, Job's children were all related to Job's wife in some respects more tenderly still than they were related to him. But the prophet recognised that it was manifestly impossible to give anything like a reasoned-out account of the difficulties in every life that should come into his narrative. He saw, however, what must be plain to us also, that in the case of Job taken as a whole, we have the great problem of the mystery of pain presented to us in the acutest possible form in which it could occur in any single life.

Here we have a good man suffering long agony, both of mind and body, and doing so with no prospect of relief but the grave, and that, too, the grave where Jesus had not yet lain. If this can be explained, then all else can. Therefore he fixes his whole attention upon the case of Job alone. And neither must we, as students of the book, suffer ourselves to be drawn aside, either in the prologue or at any later point, by the difficulties that present themselves in any side issue. The God of Job is the same God who thus reproved His servant Jonah—" Should not I spare Nineveh, that great city, wherein are more than six thousand persons, who cannot discern between their right hand and their left, and also much cattle." And if this prologue should lead us to imagine that the lives of Job's family were less sacred in the eyes of Job's God than Job's own life, it is only because we have utterly misunderstood its meaning. God's tender mercy is indeed over all His works ; but as for us, it is not only impossible for us to contemplate the whole universe at once, but we find that it is more than enough for us to understand the mysteries of one life at one time. This then is the preliminary question, and this is its sufficient answer.

We come now to the examination of the trial itself. The first part of it comes upon Job suddenly in the form of four successive blows in which the savage cruelty of men and the blind forces of nature seem banded together against the good man for his utter overthrow. But the three first blows are so similar as to form a class by themselves, and they are separated in quality by a wide difference from the last, the loss of his children, which in its unspeakably tragic significance stands quite alone.

With perfect poetic skill the scene is laid on a family feast-day of reunion in the happy spring time of the year, so that the contrast between prosperous hope and sudden awful ruin should be as deep as possible. This chosen day of festivity was, when it came, although in the spring time, a portentous day of storm and mighty wind such as is not uncommon in those desert regions of the east, when the terrific violence of the gale breaks strong trees by the trunk and drives solidly built houses into ruins—a day in which the majestic music of the thunder sounded through the darkened heavens like the trumpet of final doom, and the lightnings falling like flames of judgment from the skies consumed both the herds of cattle and the servants who were watching over them.

It was a day well suited to the ruthless work of the wild robber bands of the desert, who did not fail to take full advantage of the darkness and the storm. And as one messenger comes upon the heels of another to deliver his woeful news like a dagger thrust into the heart of the same man, we must remember that it is no life that by its wickedness has long cried aloud to God for judgment which is thus visited with overwhelming calamity, but that it is the devoted and righteous Job, a man whom God himself describes as perfect and upright, around whom all this wreck and ruin are concentrated.

" There came messengers unto Job and said, The oxen were ploughing and the asses were feeding beside them, and the Sabeans fell upon them and

TRIAL BY SUFFERING LOVE 29

took them away, yea they have slain the servants with the edge of the sword, and I only am escaped alone to tell thee. While he was yet speaking there came also another and said, The fire of God is fallen from heaven, and hath burned up the sheep and the servants and consumed them, and I only am escaped alone to tell thee. While he was yet speaking there came also another and said, The Chaldeans made out three bands and fell upon the camels, and have carried them away, yea, and slain the servants with the edge of the sword, and I only am escaped alone to tell thee." These are terrible blows. His riches have suddenly spread the wings, which they often cunningly conceal but are never without, and have disappeared. He has at once lost his all. That morning he was a princely Emeer, but now in the evening he is a beggar.

Now there are many every day subjected to similar sudden and sweeping reverses of fortune, which plunge them and their families into ruin; and judging from the effects which such trials produce, they must be terrible to bear. They have often driven men to misanthropy and madness, and have even led many to conclude after great mental agony and hopeless struggle that death was better than life.

30 AFFLICTIONS OF THE RIGHTEOUS

But what we have specially to remember here is this—that to no Christian man to-day could any such trial come with such a dark significance as these great worldly losses had for Job. For the very thing which gave its most terrible meaning to the desolation in which he found himself was the *moral* significance of his wealth in the eyes of his generation as the divine seal and approval upon the uprightness of his life. He knew at once that he would now be looked upon, even by his friends, as an unmasked hypocrite. And yet in the face of all this Job only bowed his head and worshipped, and said—" The Lord gave, and the Lord hath taken away, blessed be the name of the Lord. Naked came I out of my mother's womb, and naked shall I return thither." The sentence is slightly confused, but the meaning is plain. He shall not return to his mother's womb, but to the womb of mother earth, whither his mother has gone.

He humbly learned the lesson that a man's life consisteth not in the abundance of the things that he possesseth, but in the kind of being that he is. One thing only abides—character. What a man has departs like morning mist ; what he is remains eternally of consequence. This is the great truth on which Job first falls back for peace and comfort

TRIAL BY SUFFERING LOVE 31

in the hour of his deep need. And blessed is the man who can follow him there, for within him must be a consciousness of personal integrity, and a humble trust in the justice and goodness of God in relation to his own life. It is a good thing for a man to learn, even though he learns it through want, that the things that are seen are temporal, but the things that are unseen are eternal. It is a good thing when he learns the lesson of the flowers that neither toil nor spin and yet are arrayed in a glory greater than Solomon's. It is a good thing when he realises in his time of poverty and need that he is of more value to God than many flowers, than many sparrows, and takes home to his heart the comfort of the eternal Father's care, and remembers that the Father knoweth that he has need of all these things.

What these first three successive reports meant when taken together was that from being the richest man in all that region he was suddenly reduced to beggary. That was trial by worldly loss in its most extreme form, and Job must have felt it to be terrible indeed, especially in view of its moral meaning. But now there came to him a fourth and last messenger, whose tidings were far more awful than that of even all the three previous messengers put together. The evil news of the first three he could bear with some measure of patience and resignation, although they blotted out the golden prospect of his life as with a thick cloud; but how shall he bear the appalling words of this last and worst of all the four dreadful messengers of that most dreadful day? "Thy sons and thy daughters were eating and drinking wine in their eldest brother's house; and behold, there came a great wind from the wilderness and smote the four corners of the house, and it fell upon the young men, and they are dead; and I only am escaped alone to tell thee."

This meant something far more precious than all his worldly wealth, even the priceless treasures of his heart. Had his been a selfish and worldly heart it would have quivered less beneath these dreadful tidings. But we have seen how Job loved his children with a tender, pure, and spiritual love; and that he was the high-priest of his family, constantly interceding with sacrifices for his children, lest they should in any way go astray. He was the true father of a numerous and well-trained family, who were his joy and pride. But now he hears that his seven noble sons, and his three fair daughters, who were the light of his eyes, the brightness of his days, and the fond hope of his advancing age, have been all torn from him at one fell stroke.

How must he have felt in his heart like the aged Jacob—" If I am bereaved of my children, I am bereaved "; for just such hearts as Job's are most deeply distressed by such sorrows. What a state and prospect were his when the sun rose upon him that morning! Now, as the wild storm-clouds roll in black tumult through the gloomy west, shutting out the dim light of the swiftly descending sun and drawing on the night, how typical of his own desolate life is the darkly dying day, how changed is his state, how black are his prospects! The arrows of cruel calamity quiver in the heart of the beggared and bereaved old man. He reminds us of King Lear, left unprotected, like a poor "forked animal," to "bide the pelting of the pitiless storm," and sore amazed that the majestic forces of nature should seem to assist the cruelties of human nature in their assault upon a "head so old and white as his." The pathos of the situation is also greatly intensified by the contrast presented between the glory of the past and the desolation and sorrow of the present, for, like the ruined and bereaved Macduff, he "cannot but

c

remember that such things were, and were most precious to him."

There are many somewhat similar pages in the records of human sorrow. That is another page which records the pathetic scene at the gate of Nain, where a widow wept over the dead body of her only son; but He was there, Who is the resurrection and the Life. That is another page in which we read of the sisters of Bethany weeping because of the death of their only brother; but again He was there, to make the darkness light about them, and to give them the oil of joy for mourning, and the garment of praise for the spirit of heaviness. And pages of the same great history of sorrow are daily being filled up, pages that record the deep heart-anguish that thousands are continually passing through in their trial of suffering love. But the sombre facts are now always touched for those who have the upward eye of faith by the glory of a new light from heaven; for now the risen Saviour is ever with His followers, and will be with them to the end of the world, and His shining presence gives a new meaning to the dark and cloudy days of life. The grief that follows the death of dear ones may still well be great and deep, for the present separa-

TRIAL BY SUFFERING LOVE 35

tion is terribly complete ; but it is true that Christ has abolished the death that Job knew.

In the year 1713 the three sons of that distinguished champion of civil and religious liberty, Ebenezer Erskine, died one after another. Henry in his eighth, Alexander in his fifth, and Ralph in his second year. Very pathetic, and yet also very beautiful, are the notes in the father's diary which refer to these terrible trials. " I find," he writes after the first death, " that since the death of the child my soul has been more quickened in the way of duty than formerly, more lively in prayer, more resolved to follow the Lord, and to cleave to Him. I find that I need this spur of affliction to excite me to my duty, and it has made me more importunate on behalf of my poor child who is a-dying."

And after the second death he writes—" I have grounds of hope that my sweet Henry is now praising and triumphing with Christ in glory." And on the death of the third he writes—" I cannot express the grief of my heart for the loss of this child, the other two strokes being so recent. The Lord make me content with His dispensations, and give me the sanctified use of these repeated breaches in my poor family." After that came the crushing blow of his wife's death. After that again his fourth child died. Then he wrote —" Upon the seventh day of December, my dear, sweet, and pleasant child, Isabel Erskine, died of the small-pox . . . I take it kindly that the Lord comes to my family to gather lilies wherewith to garnish the upper sanctuary; for of such is the kingdom of heaven. And O, it sometimes affords me a pleasing prospect to think I have so much plenishing in heaven before me, and that when I enter the gates of glory, I shall not only be welcomed by the whole general assembly of saints and angels, but my wife and four pleasant babes will, in a particular manner, welcome me to these regions of glory, and I shall join in the hallelujahs of the higher house, which shall never have an end."

This well illustrates the difference that the coming of Christ has made when the shadow of death comes over the home of the godly man. Bereavement can never be to the Christian what it was to Job in that day of his overwhelming loss, for a great divine light now shines in such human darkness, and if men only comprehend it in their hearts it " turneth the shadow of death into the morning."

But now how will Job comport himself in his most awful situation ? Will Satan's prophecy be fulfilled ? That is the supreme question. The first thing Job does is to mourn, and to express his grief in signs according to the appointed manner of his time. " He arose and rent his mantle and shaved his head." This is his way of putting on mourning weeds. He is no stoic. He feels deeply, and he shows that he so feels with simple naturalness. It is well that all the mourning of religious men and women for their beloved dead should be simple, natural, true, and above all that it should be rather underdone than overdone in all its outward signs. It is well if the bereaved one can sincerely say with Hamlet :—

> " 'Tis not alone my inky cloak—
> Nor customary suits of solemn black,
> No, nor the fruitful river in the eye,
> Nor the dejected 'haviour of the visage,
> Together with all forms, moods, shows of grief,
> That can denote me truly : these indeed seem,
> For they are actions that a man might play :
> But I have that within which passeth show ;
> These but the trappings and the suits of woe."

Job mourns : and he mourns with the keen consciousness that all this has come upon him in the providence of his righteous God. With penetrating and unerring vision he sees God's hand controlling these awful events in this darkest day of his life. He has no faithless word like "chance" in his vocabulary. Behind the wild tribes of the Beduin, and behind the Chaldean hordes, and above the lightning's flash, and above the terrible storm-winds he sees—God. He knows that these dark times, like the bright times that went before them, are still in God's hand, and he says—"The Lord gave, and the Lord hath taken away."

What, then, will he say of the hand that thus smites him to the heart? "He fell down upon the ground and worshipped." This is where the saint conquers Satan, and falsifies the charge which Satan had made against him, and justifies the confidence which God had reposed in him. No man ever gets a chance of worshipping God such as he gets in some such dark day of grief. And it is in that worship alone that the comfort is to be found which avails and endures. Job bows his head and recognises the temporary nature of all man's earthly possessions, and he confesses also that God has a right to remove from his sight and touch the dearest treasures of his heart. The picture which Horace gives us of the just

TRIAL BY SUFFERING LOVE

man in overwhelming trouble is a noble one indeed :—

"Not the rage of the million commanding things evil,
Not the doom frowning near in the brows of the tyrant,
  Shakes the upright and resolute man,
  In his solid completeness of soul ;
No, not Auster, the storm-king of Hadria's wild billows,
No, not Jove's mighty hand when he launches the thunder ;
  If in fragments were shattered the world,
  Him the ruins would strike undismayed.'

But the picture presented to us here by the Hebrew prophet is nobler still. It is not poorer in fortitude, and it is richer far in humility, and in reverence, and in faith, but especially in praise. True praise is the supreme function of all God's moral creatures. But it is manifestly most worthy, as it is most difficult, when it is rendered amid circumstances of deep mystery and distress. And it was to this high quality of praise that Job attained when he uttered amid such awful desolation those sacred words—words which have so often since been used by lips that quivered with an inward agony in the same strange fellowship of vivid, aching grief—" The Lord gave, and the Lord hath taken away, blessed be the name of the Lord."

That is praise indeed. That, surely, is a great word to speak in such an hour. That word proclaims the fact that the first part of this great trial at least is a failure on the side of Satan, and a God-honouring victory on the side of Job. After all is said it is true of the vast majority of men that their days of joy are many, and that their days of grief are comparatively few. That is a reason why they should not fail in rendering the note of praise even in the day of mourning. In this aspect of that dark experience it is the godly man's great opportunity. Then may he walk with God in the fire, and then may he hold blessed fellowship with Him there, like the three Hebrew youths in the days of Daniel, if only he can say from the heart—" Blessed be the name of the Lord."

But it should be easier for Christian men to say these words after Job, because they can say them with a new and infinitely richer meaning. The Lord gave . . . blessed be the name of the Lord. " God so loved the world that He gave His only begotten Son." After that a Christian man may well believe, even when God leads him into darkest places, where he can by no means see his way, but can only feel the strength and tenderness of God's sustaining hand, that God's will is ever better than his own. Just because God's ways

TRIAL BY SUFFERING LOVE

are past finding out man's highest triumphs, when he accepts the guiding of God's will, are often, like Job's, and even like those of His own beloved Son, attained through the most terrible seeming defeats.

The Lord gave : and not all that the Lord can ever take away can overshadow the eternal glory of His great gift of Christ, but rather does that supreme gift—that unspeakable Gift—give all our loss a new and hallowed meaning and touch it with a deathless hope of life beyond the grave. It was God's will that man should know that He is love. Therefore the Lord gave—gave His beloved Christ to die for man. And shall not they who trust in Christ say over their dear dead what Job said over his ?—they who remember how Christ was "taken away," and who know how great and gracious a meaning His being taken away had for them, and for all the world—shall not they be able to say, even although with tears, yet with a loving faith in the great Father which no sorrow can destroy—" The Lord gave, and the Lord hath taken away, blessed be the name of the Lord." Shall they not be able to say with another greatly bereaved soul :—

42 AFFLICTIONS OF THE RIGHTEOUS

"'O living will that shalt endure,
 When all that seems shall suffer shock,
 Rise in the spiritual rock,
Flow through our deeds and make them pure.

That we may lift from out of dust
 A voice as unto Him that hears,
 A cry above the conquered years,
To one that with us works, and trust

With faith, that comes of self-control,
 The truths that never can be proved,
 Until we close with all we loved,
And all we flow from, soul in soul?'

CHAPTER III

TRIAL BY PHYSICAL PAIN

WE have now considered the first stage of Job's trial, and we have seen how nobly his faith in God triumphed over the severity of that terrible test, manifesting a resignation to the righteous will of God which was all the more beautiful because it was accompanied by that most sacred quality of praise which can alone rise in the darkest days of grief when its music is mingled with mourning.

We now come to the study of the second stage of this ordeal to which the suffering saint is subjected. His first trial, as we have seen, was on a great and crushing scale, both in regard to worldly loss and bereavement. In this cumulative testing he is now to be tried by personal physical pain, and this, also, as we shall see, is to be of such a kind as to take him to the utmost limit possible to human endurance.

This second stage in the proving and revelation of the high quality of the saint's faith in his God is, like the first, introduced by a remarkable scene in heaven. And here we are once more reminded of the idealising element in the book by the repetition of the self-same words in this second dialogue between God and Satan, which were used in the first dialogue, already considered. This remark, however, applies only to the first part of this second dialogue, the latter part of which is new and springs from the new situation to which our attention is now called, a situation created by the steadfast refusal of Job to succumb to Satan's temptation. The repetition of the same words, to which I have referred, may suggest that there was a considerable interval of time between Job's first and his second trial, but of this we have no definite indication in the book.

Now the first thing to note in the new part of this second scene in heaven is the divine approval of Job's conduct under trial, expressed in the words —" He still holdeth fast his integrity." This strikingly reminds us of an often unrealised, and sometimes quite forgotten truth, namely, that God Himself is the greatest of the great cloud of witnesses that encompass us around in all our moral struggles in this world. We are further reminded that He is by no means a disinterested spectator of

TRIAL BY PHYSICAL PAIN 45

our wrestling against the principalities and powers of darkness and the spiritual wickednesses in high places that war against our souls. We are reminded that God can be, and that in fact He is, most deeply moved by the manner in which we bear ourselves in that great struggle, and that He is ever ready to break forth in the praise of His creature whenever that praise is deserved, because He finds a deep pure joy, which is altogether worthy of Himself, in His creature's fidelity and love.

And how much this praise of God would mean for men if only they would seek more earnestly to estimate it at its true worth. We read of how, in the old days of Rome, hundreds of gladiators were ready to risk their lives in the arena for the sake of obtaining the transient applause of a capricious mob; we see at present in every walk of life what arduous and prolonged labours men are willing to undergo for the sake of obtaining the applause of their fellow-men, in whatever form that praise may be expressed. How far otherwise it might be if men only made their own the deep meaning which lies at the heart of that great question of Christ—" How can ye believe, which receive glory one of another, and the glory which cometh from the only God ye seek not ? " But it is conduct like Job's in the testing times of trial which proves that a man believes indeed.

But we are to note further here the form in which God's approval of His suffering servant is expressed. "And the Lord said unto Satan, Hast thou considered my servant Job? for there is none like him in the earth, a perfect and an upright man, one that feareth God, and escheweth evil; and he still holdeth fast his integrity, although thou movedst me against him, to destroy him without cause." The phrase, "he still holdeth fast his integrity" brings into view the moral aspect of the temptation. The emphasis is laid, not upon the grief Job feels under his terrible losses, nor upon the beautiful humility of spirit with which he accepts these from God's hands, nor even the praise which he offers to God in his dark hour, but it is laid upon the way in which Job relates his losses to his own moral character.

He does not accept these losses as conclusive proofs that he is a sinner above all men, he does not acknowledge that the magnitude of the disasters that have come upon him is a revelation of the measure of his secret sinfulness and of God's condemnation of his moral character. No, he holds fast to his integrity; his innocence, he feels, must

TRIAL BY PHYSICAL PAIN 47

be maintained against all such unjust inferences as these; he will not be false to the truth in order to square the facts with the orthodox teaching of the time, which hitherto he has himself also believed.

Though he is profoundly perplexed and deeply distressed by the strange moral contradictions of the fearful position in which he finds himself he is prepared to stand by the truth although the heavens fall, he will still hold fast his integrity; and it is a very noteworthy fact, and one of extraordinary importance, that it is for *this* above all else that God commends him and makes his boast of him to Satan.

But having first approved the conduct of his suffering servant, God next reproaches Satan. "Thou movedst me against him to destroy him without cause." Here we have an example of the difficulty of expressing in human modes the ways and thoughts of God. It is not intended to be suggested by these words that God is less than absolute master of his own will, nor that His purposes come to Him, as it were, at second-hand from any outside source, least of all from any evil source. To destroy a man without cause would evidently be a moral wrong. It is inconceivable that God could ever be moved to do any such thing. As the Apostle James says—"God cannot be tempted with evil, and He Himself tempteth no man."

The divine reproach of Satan here refers to the groundlessness of Satan's first insinuation as to the character of Job's religion. It indicates the base part which has been played by Satan in this whole matter, and suggests that this has been proved by the way in which Job has triumphed in the trial to which he has been subjected by God having accepted the challenge addressed to Him by Satan. God had suffered the test, not because He was in any doubt as to what the result would be, but for the sake of two entirely worthy ends, namely, for the manifestation of the truth and trust which he knew to be in the heart of His servant, and also for the unmasking of this evil which he also knew to be in the heart of Satan. For the reproach of God sets forth the malignity of Satan, and it shows that God remembers the malice of the devil as well as the integrity and faithfulness of His servant, and thus it makes very plain which side God stands on in this great battle between good and evil.

But in the answer of Satan to God we are shown that evil works in Satan as it does everywhere else and "grows by what it feeds on." He has now

TRIAL BY PHYSICAL PAIN

a new insinuation to offer against Job, which is baser even than the first. The truth is that evil cannot endure goodness, and is maddened by its very presence, and most of all when it successfully resists the malign influences which would stain it and degrade it.

Therefore Satan hisses out the new lie which is so true to the spirit of evil. "Skin for skin," he says, "yea, all that a man hath will he give for his life. But put forth thine hand now and touch his bone and his flesh, and he will renounce thee to thy face." The first part of this answer of Satan is probably an ancient proverb. The meaning seems to be that men will readily come and go with comparatively little concern in regard to all external troubles, but that the only sufficient test of a man is when some fearful calamity invades the circle of his own personal life. Whether this is true in any individual case, however, depends entirely upon the character of the man who is being tried.

In this second base assertion concerning Job, Satan further reveals the evil of his own nature, and also his own utter incapacity to appreciate the possibilities that lie in a lofty nature. He so utterly misunderstands the heart of Job that he is

D

confident that personal physical pain will prove a more terrible thing to him than the awful sorrows of bereavement which he has already suffered. But it is evident that to such a heart as Job's extreme physical pain could only be a greater trial in view of its being added to all that had gone before, and in view of the profound moral significance of all these things as affecting his relation to God, and as affecting the estimation in which he was held by good men. For, as Dr Watson finely says,—"Human love has divine depths which a sneering devil cannot see."

"Put forth thine hand now and touch his bone and his flesh, and he will renounce thee to thy face." This is Satan's second challenge. "Behold, he is in thine hand," is the divine reply. God knows His servant; and if His servant can trust Him, so He can trust His servant. But we are again reminded of the complete subjection of Satan to God in all his evil operations against Job by the added words—"Only spare his life." The new liberty of Satan is large, but this is its final restriction. And we are to remember that there is always a restriction appointed by divine love and power when Satan is permitted to trouble the servants of God; and even when life is not spared, as is

TRIAL BY PHYSICAL PAIN 51

often the case, death marks the utmost limit of trial for all troubled souls who are faithful to the end; for beyond this point trial ends and is transformed to everlasting victory.

That is why it was perfectly reasonable for Christ to say to his disciples as they were going forth to face the most deadly persecution for His name's sake—" And I say unto you my friends, Be not afraid of them which kill the body, and after that have no more that they can do. But I will warn you whom ye shall fear: fear him which after he hath killed hath power to cast into hell; yea, I say unto you, fear him."

These words of Christ ask His disciples to contemplate the extreme experience of martyrdom for His name's sake, and to do this quite calmly, with the firm assurance that life in the body is a little thing in comparison with the great life that follows, and that beyond death the powers of evil cannot pursue them. The only thing that is worthy of being feared by the godly man is the degradation of character and the moral judgments that inevitably follow that. Death itself is nothing to that, because it is that alone which arms death with all its most terrible powers.

We are now brought face to face with the great

problem of human pain as it is presented to us in the case of Job—that is to say, in its most perplexing possible form. "So Satan went forth from the presence of the Lord and smote Job." And what a smiting that was! The more we consider it the more clearly we see that in respect to physical pain as well as in regard to worldly loss and bereavement the case of Job is typical and extreme.

His malady was the worst form of leprosy. It was sometimes called elephantiasis, because of the frightful condition to which it reduced the skin, and sometimes it was called "the botch of Egypt," because it was most frequently seen in that country. It was always a fearful disease in any of its forms, but we gather from the terrible details given in the subsequent chapters of the book that in the case of Job its malignity reached a perfect climax. We find that it was attended with frightful ulcers, and most distressing itching, with inward corruption such as made the very breath a fetid pestilence, with swollen limbs and horribly corrugated skin.

Nor was even this all. We learn also that Job's sores bred worms and gave forth a most loathsome smell—that the disease frequently induced sensations of choking—that it was accompanied by gnawing pain which he felt like a fire burning

TRIAL BY PHYSICAL PAIN 53

within his bones—and that if at any time his exhaustion from pain brought sleep he was then, even during such brief respite from more extreme agony, harrowed by frightful dreams. In most cases of leprosy only a part of the body is affected by the fell disease, but Job was smitten with it from the crown of the head to the sole of the feet.

He was so disfigured by it that even his familiar friends could not recognise him; and it made him so offensive that he was carried out and laid upon the mound of ashes called the "mezbele," that is the name given to the place where the refuse of an eastern village is burned, and which is the common refuge of beggars and outcasts. None cared to approach him, but all were disposed to shun him, and yet he was so helpless as scarcely to be able to rise from the spot where he lay. Who can wonder that in such a condition he longed for death as for the one possible blessing; and yet such was the nature of the disease that while there was no hope left for the sufferer of any restoration to health he might continue to exist in this appalling state even for years.

Now if we remember all the trial and sorrow which preceded this visitation in the experience

54   AFFLICTIONS OF THE RIGHTEOUS

of Job, we shall, I think, readily allow, as we look upon this pitiful human wreck that this man has reached the uttermost point of misery conceivable by us. The sufferings of an innocent little child might seem at first sight even more mysterious to us. But the very innocence which, on a superficial view, might dispose us to think so, is the very thing which makes such a case less and not more mysterious than that of Job.

The radical difference is that the child is innocent rather than righteous. It has not yet been called to endure the strain of moral choice. Moreover, the child is not exposed to such trials as those which Job has already passed through : he cannot be cast down from the height of prosperity, nor can he know, as Job has already known, the sorrows of bereavement. Finally, and very specially, he has not a man's mind nor a man's soul to understand and to feel the terribleness of the situation either from the human or from the divine side. But all these things were great and important factors in the agonies of Job.

But the supreme question that now arises and presses for solution in presence of such a situation is this—What now, in face of this terrible spectacle of a good man under such overwhelming

TRIAL BY PHYSICAL PAIN 55

disaster and sorrow and pain, is to be said of the favourite orthodox doctrine of Job's time, and which still held its place centuries after Job's time, that prosperity is the divine seal of virtue ?

And let us be careful to note here again the intense modern interest of this problem, although to us it may have changed its aspect somewhat. The fact is that the ancients were wiser than we moderns with regard to this question, in this respect, that while they regarded God's approval as the supreme good of life, and prosperity as its sign, very many of us now hold, or what really matters much more, live as though we held, that prosperity and its accompanying enjoyments are in themselves the supreme good of life.

It is added, therefore, that pain is an evil and can be nothing else ; and men have so argued about this as to make it plain that in both directions they have mistaken the means for the end. For this false conception of pain and pleasure has even been exalted to the dignity of a philosophy of life, and John Stuart Mill has frankly subscribed to it, and Herbert Spencer has expounded it with most voluminous learning, and to crown all Schopenhauer, the German pessimist, has espoused it with such extravagant energy as to render his pleading sometimes tragic, and sometimes grotesque.

But we cannot be too thankful that there still have been given to the world, even in these last times also, seers, men of truer and purer vision, whose outlook has wider horizons and whose perceptions are both more comprehensive and more penetrating because they are more spiritual. And one of these seers has sung to us a psalm of life, simple, and yet so strong and deep and true that it has made its echo clearly heard over all the mingled shoutings and wailings of the world—

> "Not enjoyment and not sorrow,
> Is our destined end or way,
> But to act that each to-morrow
> Finds us further than to-day."

And another, with a still mightier voice, has sung to us again—

> "Is it for nothing we grow old and weak,
> We whom God loves? When pain ends gain ends too."

And yet another of the same high fellowship of spiritual genius, who sang out of the depths of long experience of pain, has made this strong appeal to us, tender, and yet so severe—

TRIAL BY PHYSICAL PAIN 57

"O brothers, let us leave the shame and sin
Of taking vainly, in a plaintive mood,
The holy name of grief-holy herein,
That by the grief of One came all our good."

And yet one more great soul has given us this most beautiful and most refining song, worthy to be sung through all the coming years together with the other three in every house of pain and trial and sorrow—

"Some murmur when their sky is clear
  And wholly bright to view,
If one small speck of dark appear
  In their great heaven of blue:
And some with thankful love art filled,
  If but one streak of light,
One ray of God's good mercy, gild
  The darkness of their night."

In such songs as these we have both sides of the human response to the trials and troubles which are assigned to men in this world. Surely the majority of men are too prone to make a great noise about the smaller troubles of life, and comparatively few of us are as thankful as we should be for our common "Great heaven of blue."

But in the study of Job's case our business is rather with the deep darkness than with the

58 AFFLICTIONS OF THE RIGHTEOUS

brightness, or even with the lighter shades of life. And truly it is a deep and terrible darkness that spreads over multitudes of human lives because of the cloud of physical pain; and the trial which it involves cannot by any means be confined to those who suffer immediately in their own bodies; for the members of one family are indeed members one of another, and if one member suffer all the other members suffer with it. When the angel of pain visits one he casts the dark shadow of his presence over all the rest, and they too have to endure hardship and trouble and anxiety.

Much of the suffering that is in the world is thus mediate, and is caused by the condition of some one life so near and dear to others that their experiences cannot be taken wholly apart from each other. The aspects which this complex problem of pain takes are very various, and some of them are much more perplexing than others. A sharp and critical illness, severe while it lasts but swiftly passing away, is one of its more common forms. It has a much more mysterious aspect when it comes to us in the form of a protracted malady, which involves acute suffering, which brings a man down to

TRIAL BY PHYSICAL PAIN 59

the very gates of death, and from which he is allowed even at last to make so imperfect a recovery that in one way or another his life is permanently maimed or limited in a way it had never been before.

More mysterious still is the aspect which pain wears when a conspicuously good man is called upon to suffer greatly through a long period on account of his very goodness, and with no prospect of any deliverance but that which death would bring, as has been the case with many of those noble souls that have won the martyr's crown. But surely the very crown and climax of this deep mystery of human pain is reached in the case of Job, in which we have a true saint after he had just been overwhelmed by other appalling troubles, required to undergo extreme physical agony, long drawn out, with death as the only termination of it for which he could hope, but above all, and most terrible of all in regard to which all men, even his nearest and dearest friends, recognised in those very agonies he was enduring the divine condemnation of his life as that of an unmasked sinner— a condemnation which his own soul rejected with indignation because he felt it to be utterly unjust. Here, surely, you have the great and many-sided mystery of pain at its densest and darkest.

I happen to know much about this mystery or pain from terribly close contact with it and observation of it in great infirmaries, in incurable homes, and in those strange human dens, so unworthy of the name of Home, and which Tennyson has justly described as " the warrens of the poor." And I would not seek to minimise it as is sometimes done, nor would I talk lightly of it as if it were a thing of comparatively small account, or as if the shortness of this life can be regarded as a sufficient explanation of it. No, I think we must make frank recognition of it in all its terribleness. Never by any vain, stoical endeavour to treat human pain as if it were not, or as if it were one of the minor things of life, can we ever rise superior to its power.

And still less can we by any such means obtain from it the moral and spiritual discipline which it is fitted and intended to provide for us. It is imposssible to believe that a good and loving God has any satisfaction in the suffering of the creature whom He loves for the mere sake of the suffering. We cannot believe this even when it is granted

TRIAL BY PHYSICAL PAIN 61

that the creature is bad; for what is the badness of the creature but the foil of the goodness of the Creator, who is also the Saviour?

If then, this good God, who is also almighty, does not deliver His creature from suffering, it can only be, either because there is some moral impossibility involved, in relation to the free self-determination of the creature, in the exercise of which the creature clings to that which entails suffering, and does so against the will of God, or it must be because the temporary pain is the necessary means by which alone the creature can attain to the highest and most enduring state, both of being and of blessing.

Now it is this latter alternative which has been to many the supreme test of their faith in God. We know that many a bad man's sins bring suffering to him, and it is easy to see that in so suffering he suffers righteously. But when a most saintly man suffers, as Job suffered, for some end which we can by no means clearly see, then, indeed, may both faith and patience have their perfect work. This is the nature of the problem as it is set before us in this great book. We see that the special temptation of the man in such a situation is always to revolt against Him under whose rule he suffers so much and so mysteriously. But blessed be the God and Father of our Lord Jesus Christ there is now a great Light shining in this darkness, though often it is still sadly true that the darkness comprehendeth it not—

> "So many hearts are crushed and torn,
>   So many lives are full of woe,
> We sometimes ask—Should such be born,
>   If they must weep and sorrow so?
>
> Yet, Winter but prepares for Spring,
>   Day breaks from the dark womb of Night,
> The seed must die, ere it can bring
>   The flower within it into light.
>
> Out of the storm the rainbow gleams,
>   The grub precedes the beauteous fly—
> Man shall not be what now he seems
>   When God completes him by and bye.
>
> We ask—Can God be Lord of Love,
>   And also Lord of sov'reign power,
> Yet look in silence from above,
>   While hearts are breaking every hour?
>
> So question we, nor apprehend
>   Our questions answered long ago,
> When God His best Beloved did send,
>   To make His own our deepest woe.
>
> And He, the world's one perfect Man,
>   Was only perfected by pain,

TRIAL BY PHYSICAL PAIN

Revealing love and power that can
 By loss achieve the greatest gain.

Ah ! yes, God's heavens most grandly glow
 When night reveals each shining star ;
We need our darkest hours to know
 How great His tender mercies are."

CHAPTER IV

JOB'S WIFE AND FRIENDS

Job's wife presents but a sorry figure in this book. The lines in which her character is drawn are few but they are firm and definite. Augustine described her as "diaboli adjutrix"—Satan's assistant. In a similar way the great Greek father, Chrysostom, held that when Satan destroyed all the other members of Job's family he spared his wife, because he knew that she would be specially useful to him in his temptation of Job.

But whatever may be said of these interpretations of her relation to the work of Satan, it is clear from the narrative that the religion of Job's wife was exactly of that false commercial kind which Satan described as the religion of Job himself when he asserted that severe trial would transform him from a worshipper into a blasphemer of God. This appears from the evil council which she gives her husband in the dark hour when

JOB'S WIFE AND FRIENDS

most he needed from her true comfort and noble inspiration.

"Dost thou still hold fast thy integrity?" she asks, "renounce God and die." It was well to worship God when the gifts of God were good, but she was amazed that Job should continue holding fast to a profitless, if not to a cruel God. Ewald truly says—"Nothing can be more scornful than her words, which mean—Thou, who under all the undeserved sufferings which have been inflicted on thee by thy God hast been faithful to Him, even in fatal sickness, as if He would help, or desired to help, thee who art beyond help; to thee, fool, I say, bid God farewell, and die."

Now it is of great importance at this point that we should endeavour to see clearly the broad bearings of the whole situation in which Job finds himself in order that we may be the better able to understand the important difference between the position of Job's wife and that of his three friends in relation to his great trial, and what that means in the subsequent debate.

The fundamental assumption of all four is that

prosperity is the seal of the divine approval on the moral conduct of the prosperous one, and that pain and disaster indicate the reverse. Therefore they argue that if in the providence of God special distress comes upon a man either he is unrighteous, or God is unjust. This is a position with regard to which they are all of one mind.

But then, Job's wife knew the integrity of her husband as none of his friends could know it. If a man's wife believes him perfect, then he is perfect. Job's wife was familiar with all the private details of his life; and many a time these, we may be sure, had filled such a woman as she was with wonder and admiration, and had put her to secret shame. If God pronounced that life "perfect" she could do no less; not because she believed in God, but simply because she knew the facts. But because she was without her husband's faith, therefore her conventional orthodoxy drove her to take sides with him against God. Since her husband was certainly righteous God must be unjust, and so should be renounced. She therefore viewed her husband as a good but foolish man—a credulous, religious fanatic.

JOB'S WIFE AND FRIENDS

The three friends of Job, on the other hand, not knowing his life and character so intimately as his wife did, and arguing from the same assumption as she did, concluded that there must be some secret iniquity in the life of Job in order to account for the terrible calamities that overwhelmed him, and so they took sides with God and against Job. They did this at first with great reluctance, for all that they had known of Job in the past years of their friendship had disposed them to believe in him firmly as a good and upright man, but now to their minds his awful troubles formed strong evidence to the contrary.

They could see no way to any other conclusion than that Job was in reality a very different kind of man from what they had believed him to be, and although in the early part of the discussion they show their sympathy with the sufferer and the difficulty which they have in taking this new and adverse view of their old friend, yet in the latter part of the debate they grow hardened and even cruel in their condemnation of him, and allow themselves even to make specific charges of wrongdoing against him, for which they had no better foundation than their own imagination and the needs of their conventional theory of the moral order of the world.

Now the view which Job himself took of this position in relation to God was essentially different from the view that was taken of it either by his wife, or by his friends. He knew that his wife and his friends were both partly right, but only partly right. He was certain that he was not being afflicted more than all other men simply because he was more wicked than all other men; but neither, on the other hand, could he bring himself to doubt the goodness of God. He felt that he was bound to hold fast to both of these pillars of the truth with an equally tenacious grasp. He maintained his own integrity, but on the other hand, he desired to maintain with equal stedfastness that God was just. So also while he denied that God was unjust he could not deny his own integrity, as the accepted orthodoxy of the time required him to do. It is the agonising struggle after a full reconciliation between these seeming opposites in the mind of Job, who *alone* sees the whole problem fully, which forms the great theme of the book.

JOB'S WIFE AND FRIENDS 69

Now the beauty of Job's character is further revealed in the answer which he gives to his wife's temptation. "Thou speakest," he says, "as one of the foolish women speaketh. What! Shall we receive good at the hand of God, and shall we not receive evil?" In this answer there is united a great tenderness and an equal faithfulness towards his wife. There is also in it a great faith and patience towards his God. We feel that it is a very noble answer in such circumstances.

We are to observe that he defends only the point which is attacked, not his own integrity—he shall defend that also afterwards when it, too, is assailed—but the mysterious providence of God, which he himself finds so hard to bear, and also so impossible to understand. His answer exposes all the base selfishness of his wife's suggestion, and yet it does so tenderly. For we must not fail to see all the concentration of pain involved in the fact that it was she, the companion of his past, and the mother of his dear dead children, who had become his temptress. And so the words—"Thou speakest as one of the foolish women speaketh," convey the idea that Job desired to think of her evil words as being unlike and unworthy of herself. And it was just this that made it so hard to hear such words from such lips at such a time.

Yet Job felt that if his wife failed in this great trial, although she was called to bear only a lesser part in it, he must not therefore fail. If his own wife will no longer worship God with him, then he must worship God alone. Like a later psalmist the language of his heart was this—" Whom have I in heaven but Thee, and there is none upon the earth that I desire beside Thee." He feels that the fellowship of his God is dearer to him yet than that of any creature, even although that creature be his wife. He will reprove her evil counsel and hold fast to God amid all the mystery and the pain, even while his heart is breaking.

He is true to the great test of Christ long before it has yet been given—" He that loveth wife or children more than me is not worthy of me." And how then must God love this man thus witnessing for him! We feel as we consider all its meaning that the answer of Job is enough on the human side. It is surely a great triumph of faith to be able to say—

JOB'S WIFE AND FRIENDS 71

"I praise Thee while my days go on,
I love Thee while my days go on,
Through dark and death, through fire and frost,
With emptied arms and treasure lost,
I thank Thee while my days go on."

We may well put these words of Mrs Browning into the mouth of Job at this crisis of his life, for they so well express his spirit that they seem but an expansion of his answer.

And yet that answer alone, while it conclusively proves the splendid faith of Job, would not vindicate the character of God against the charge of caprice, or even something worse. We have a fuller answer than this to the whole problem in which Job found himself involved from the divine voice that speaks out of the whirlwind; but even that, we feel, is not enough to meet the greatness of the need. And the final explanation of the great mystery of pain came, as it only could come, by Jesus Christ. He taught mankind that the supreme gain and loss is not pleasure and pain, but life and death. He said—"I am come that they might have life, and that they might have it more abundantly." This is really the deepest need of men, if only we understand truly what life is—

72 AFFLICTIONS OF THE RIGHTEOUS

> " 'Tis life whereof our nerves are scant,
> O life, not death for which we pant,
> More life, and fuller, that we want."

Christ further said that the fundamental assumption of the old time that prosperity was the seal of virtue, and pain and poverty were the reverse, was false. He declared that to the poor the gospel was preached. He said that a man's life consisteth not in the abundance of the things that he possesseth, but in the thing that he is. He said—" Blessed are they that mourn, for they shall be comforted." He said—" Blessed are the meek, for they shall inherit the earth." He said that a man is sometimes called to suffer, not for any sin which either he or his parents have done, but that the work of God may be made manifest in him.

And in all this, and in much more than all this, Christ himself was the embodiment and the supreme illustration of His own teaching. For He himself also suffered amid darkness and unspeakable mental agony, arising from most bewildering mystery, by reason of the challenge which the strange facts of His experience presented to His moral sense in relation to God's care over His life. And surely one great purpose of Christ's suffering

JOB'S WIFE AND FRIENDS 73

so was to show His followers how they might bear themselves worthily in the darkest days of their lives as children of the same Father.

> " By anguish which made pale the sun
> I hear Him charge His saints that none
> Among his creatures anywhere
> Blaspheme against Him in despair,
> However darkly days go on."

This ancient problem of human suffering will come back upon us again and again, as it has always done; and in life's wildest, darkest hours the old temptation to renounce God and die will be suggested to us afresh by some evil tongues from without, or it will come to us more subtly by some evil thoughts from within. But we have now, in eternal outline at least, the final and sufficient answer which establishes the reasonableness of our abiding faith in the benevolence of the divine purpose concerning our life, amid all its mystery of pain and sin and sorrow.

For who alone can claim to be the greatest sufferer among the sons of men? Is it not He who wore the crown of thorns, and who won for Himself that wondrous name—" The Man of sorrows?" And what was the net result, nay, what is still unquestionably the ever-ripening fruit which continues to spring out of all His sufferings, and not only with regard to men, but also with regard to Himself? Did those sufferings of His, which were so awful beyond all comparison with those of other men, ultimately dim His glory? Did they in any real sense narrow His life? Did they limit or impair His power either with God or with men? Did they in the end frustrate His dearest, highest hopes? Did they in any wise finally blossom out into enduring darkness or bear the fruits of any abiding misery?

Is it not rather the supreme hope and glory of the human race that they accomplished, and that they are still continuing to accomplish, precisely the reverse? For it was by His sufferings that Christ was Himself made perfect in all the fulness of His blessed manhood. It was by His sufferings that He revealed the Father, and glorified the Father, as He could never otherwise have been revealed and glorified. It was by His sufferings that He won, and is still winning, the hearts of men; for it was only by being lifted up upon the Cross that He began to draw all men unto Himself.

JOB'S WIFE AND FRIENDS 75

And therefore Jesus Christ, with the heavenly fruits of His divinely-human suffering, alone gives us the great divine answer to the mystery of human pain. If we do not find it sufficient for us it can only be because it is so exceedingly great that we cannot wholly understand it yet. But surely we may well believe, beyond our imperfect understanding, that that magnificently divine answer will completely swallow up all our doubtful questionings at last, and that by the very sufferings of life the love of God will vindicate itself to our minds and commend itself to our hearts also. Thus it certainly was in the life of the Man, Christ Jesus, and why then may it not be so in our life also, especially as His experience gives us so wonderful an interpretation of the divine end of suffering, and of its marvellous possibilities for man's highest good as well as for God's greatest glory ?

Now in the study of this great book of Job it is well for us to keep ever before our minds the answer which Christ has given to the problem of human pain. But, on the other hand, we must never forget that this great answer was hidden from the mind of the suffering Job. And if, in his awful situation, his faith was seriously tested by the conduct of his wife, it was still more seriously tested by the behaviour and the reasonings of his three friends.

In several respects these friends are very similar to each other; but when we carefully consider them we find that they have each well-marked characteristics, so that they are all distinguished by a certain individuality which reflects itself in their different arguments.

Eliphaz, the Temanite, is probably the oldest of the three; and we gather from his speeches that he is a man of rich and varied experience. He shows himself to be also possessed of a most kindly and sympathetic nature; and in his first expostulations with Job he reveals a great deal of gentleness and considerateness, both in reproving what he conceives to be the errors of his friend, and in the exhortations by which he seeks to bring him into what he thinks would be a better state of mind.

We recognise Eliphaz to be also a man of deep earnestness, so that although he is keenly sensitive to the great sufferings of his friend he cannot refrain from administering to him the rebuke which he is convinced he greatly needs for his own highest good.

But the great weakness of Eliphaz is the narrowness of his religious outlook which leads him to adopt a very contracted view both of the divine government and of man's duty, and renders him incapable of addressing himself with a worthy freedom of mind to those more difficult aspects of God's providence which are so intimately connected with the most mysterious elements of human experience. He is sure, far too sure, that his conventional theory of the divine rule is the only right one, and so it is the very earnestness of the man which leads him at last to adopt as facts his own suppositions against Job, because he feels that whatever happens God must be justified, and he wrongly persuades himself that this cannot possibly be done in any other way. This is what explains the remarkable contrast between the kindly sympathy of the first speech of Eliphaz and the sorrowful severity of his last one.

Bildad the Shuhite, on the other hand, is the type of the man of learning and research, rich in traditional lore, and with some philosophical talent also, which leads him into various speculations in support of his own position. But we do not find in him either the fulness of sympathy, or the rich experience, or the prophetic touch which we find in Eliphaz.

He is a great student of the past, and his whole nature is rooted and grounded in the authority of the past over the present. He has an open contempt for anything that savours of novelty, especially in the moral and spiritual sphere. He has more than a dash of optimism in his composition, and he treasures in his heart the hope that in the end all will come right with his erring friend; and yet his mind is full of weird pictures of what must happen to the man who would shake the foundations of human society by venturing to introduce some new ideas as to the ways of God with men.

He thinks that the only right attitude for men is to sit humbly at the feet of those who have lived before them, and to accept without question whatsoever they have to teach them; but the idea that each successive generation has a responsibility to make for itself some progress in the discovery of truth, so that it may teach in its turn to those who follow not merely what has been handed down to it but also something in addition which it has won for itself and for them—any

JOB'S WIFE AND FRIENDS 79

such idea as that was quite foreign to the mind of Bildad.

Zophar the Naamathite, again, is the representative of the orthodox dogmatic theologian of the obscurantist type, who is rigidly convinced that his system of the government of the universe admits of no improvement, and who even grows angry, quite furious indeed, with anyone who ventures to suggest that it might possibly be otherwise, and who points out clearly the moral anomalies which that theory involves. He also is Job's friend, and he is quite sincere and faithful; but he is also, like so many other friends, sometimes hard and harsh to the point of cruelty in the interest of his cast-iron theory of religion, which is a cold and crushing load to the quivering heart of his friend.

Zophar does not seek to adapt his creed to the established facts of life, but rather seeks to force the facts to fit his creed. It is always this type of religious man who has least knowledge and fails first in argument, as Zophar does. He begins with easy assurance and beaming hopefulness, because he does not see the deep gravity of the questions involved. He is angered at the suggestion of the imperfection of a creed which he would not dream of modifying, and he tries to end difficulties by unjust dogmatic assertions which have nothing but pure assumption to support them.

"Should thy lies make men hold their peace," he cries, "and when thou mockest shall no man make thee ashamed? Know therefore that God exacteth of thee less than thine inquity deserveth." And when this last refuge of cruel libel is proved to be less than sufficient to meet the needs of his theory he makes no apology; and he is silent at last, not because he is convinced, nor because he is ashamed, but because he cannot answer as he still wishes to answer, and because he gives up the man whom his words have so cruelly wounded as being a reprobate beyond all hope. And how often do we see this same arrogant, uncharitable, religious intolerance at work in our own time, even within the limits of a single Christian congregation, and often with most cruel results to many most tender and earnest hearts.

Now the great mistake which all the three friends of Job made in their judgment of his character was that their judgment was outward rather than inward; it was built upon what they saw in his surroundings, rather than on what they knew of the man himself. But, as Balzac truly says— "If you are to judge a man you must know his secret thoughts, sorrows, and feelings; to know merely the outward events of a man's life would only serve to make a chronological table—a fool's notion of history."

Now this was exactly what Job's friends persisted in doing. They would not judge him by his secret thoughts and feelings, often most earnestly and even passionately expressed, nor would they judge him by what they had known of his consistent life and character through long years of close friendship; but they would judge him, and they did judge him, notwithstanding all his agonising protests, by his altered outward circumstances in relation to their own preconceived theories of the providential order of the world. They were all three good earnest men, and also men who together represented the highest culture of their time; and yet they often in the course of this great debate speak wrong words on highest themes, and speak them, too, with the greatest confidence, as if they embodied first principles of a universal religion from which there could be no possible appeal.

Now it is because these things are true concerning the three friends of Job that there is no book in the Bible in the study of which we more deeply need the guidance of the Holy Spirit, in order to make careful and intelligent discrimination between things that fundamentally differ, than in the case of this book of Job. There is a deplorably common, loose way of quoting the Bible, in which passages are taken simply at random and made to support false positions, as if with divine authority. This is as pernicious and as subversive of primary moral distinctions as it is common; and this remark applies with peculiar propriety to this particular book.

The speeches of Job's friends should by no means be quoted, as they very often are quoted, as if they were the veritable oracles of God. No doubt these speeches contain much profound wisdom, and much deep truth; but they are so far from being all wisdom and all truth that many parts of them are really deep error. The speeches are made quite sincerely, but their arguments are often false to the very core, and if we accepted them they would inevitably lead us to conclusions diametrically opposed to the truth in regard to some of the deepest and most important things

JOB'S WIFE AND FRIENDS 83

in human life. Hence at the close of the book, when the divine verdict is given upon the whole discussion, God himself twice over declares to the three friends in two successive verses—" Ye have not spoken of Me the thing that is right, as my servant Job hath."

Now not only should we ever remember this divine verdict in all our quoting and study of this book, but we should remember the exact terms of it. For I do not know anything more suggestive in all this suggestive book than the fact that in these words the thing which God condemns is not what they have said about Job but what they have said about Himself. They had condemned Job; they had spoken many cruel and bitter and crushing words to him about himself, and the further the great debate went on the harsher and the more cruel had their condemnation of Job become, and yet God says never a word about that, He entirely passes by all that. But how had they spoken about God? Why, they had praised God from first to last—they had again and again wounded the heart of Job most terribly in order that they might still go on praising God, and that they might justify His ways with Job as they conceived of these ways. And it is of this that God speaks; it is this that He cannot pass by, and of which He so sternly complains; it is this which demands a sacrifice of which this very Job, with his wounded heart which God Himself has now bound up, must be the priest.

Here we are surely made to see, and to see clearly, that God will reject, and will reject with indignation, every man's efforts to call darkness light and light darkness that he may seek in his own foolish and false ways to justify God's dealings with men. We have here a strong warning that God will suffer no man to whitewash His providence. If there is mystery—and there is sometimes great mystery—in that providence, no man is at liberty to invent equivocations in order to explain it away, and to practically deny the facts in playing the part of divine apologist; but rather it becomes every man simply to confess the mystery and his own ignorance, and to learn to possess his soul in patience while he humbly waits for the divine explanation, which alone can ever be sufficient. Otherwise, God shall certainly condemn his false and feeble interpretation of His own great ways, which are high above man's as the heavens are above the earth, and He will also condemn the man himself for his presumptuous and dogmatic ignorance that dared to offer itself, as the sufficient champion of Omniscience.

> "God is His own interpreter,
> And He will make it plain."

CHAPTER V

JOB'S LAMENT OF LIFE

WE have now watched Job through a succession of troubles which appeared to be overwhelming; and yet we have seen that the true and just verdict upon his behaviour was this—" In all this Job sinned not, nor charged God with foolishness." And again—" In all this did not Job sin with his lips."

With the opening words of this third chapter, however, we immediately see that a great change has come over Job. " After this, Job opened his mouth and cursed his day." That is the introduction to the wild and passionate outpouring of his soul that follows, and as we go on reading his terrible lament of life we feel as if the wonderful patience and resignation which had hitherto characterised him amid his fearful trials have utterly given way, and given place to impatience and despair.

What then, has happened within the short interval of a week to produce so great a change in Job's

JOB'S LAMENT OF LIFE

attitude towards his troubles? To this question there seems but one possible answer. Job's three special bosom friends have arrived, and their whole bearing and manner towards him, even although they have not yet spoken a word, has pressed home upon his very soul the terrible moral interpretation of his calamities which he had feared would be given by men. This interpretation he himself knew to be utterly false; and yet he saw only too plainly by their behaviour that it was supported by all three of his peculiar friends with a cruel and crushing unanimity which was to him bitter exceedingly. And yet he felt it to be a verdict from which he had no appeal, save to his own conscience, and to the silent and invisible God, whose strange dealings with him seemed most powerfully to argue that He also was ranged on the side of his friends and against his suffering servant.

What view are we to take, then, of the behaviour of these friends of Job? This is a most important question; and a great deal depends upon the answer which we give to it. For there is nothing more necessary to our proper understanding of even the main intention, as well as the detailed arguments of this great book, than that we should have a fair and adequate, and not a mean and unworthy, conception of the conduct of Job's three friends.

The popular estimate of their character and conduct is lamentably inaccurate, and even unjust. It is true that they came to comfort Job; and yet they did not comfort him, but the very reverse. This one fact is fixed upon as if it were the only fact worth considering in the whole matter; and all other facts which would explain it and give to it its true interpretation are quite forgotten. For the real reason why Job's three friends did not comfort him most people never see at all, so that these men are commonly held up to scorn and condemnation as men who cruelly abused a friend in his time of overwhelming trouble when he most deeply needed their help.

But this is a most distorted view of the whole situation presented to us in the book. For we must remember that if Job's friends failed to comfort him it was just because they were true to their convictions; and it was precisely because Job knew this that their words and bearing towards himself had such terrible power to move him. We must admit that they say many things which we cannot accept as the true interpretation of Job's experi-

JOB'S LAMENT OF LIFE 89

ence ; but they can never be accused of insincerity, and there is nothing more evident during the whole course of the great debate than their earnest desire to convince Job of what they themselves believe to be the truth.

Moreover, there are many modern comforters who lightly condemn Job's friends who might nevertheless learn much that would be most valuable to the sufferers whom they approach, both from the conduct and from the words of these men. It is well said in " Mark Rutherford "—" Who that knows what modern consolation is can prevent a prayer that Job's comforters may be his ? They do not call upon him for an hour and invent excuses for the departure which they so anxiously await ; they do not write notes to him and go about their business as if nothing had happened. They do not inflict upon him meaningless commonplaces." All suffering and sorrowing souls know that the one supreme and absolutely necessary quality in a comforter is sincere sympathy. And he who fails to see that all Job's three friends had this supreme quality in a most marked degree is no fit judge of their conduct.

How did they prove the quality of their sympathy ? Away across the barren desert, at no great distance from each other, but probably about two hundred miles away from Job, they heard in their several dwelling-places of the terrible calamities which had befallen their old friend. They did not plead the distance, nor even, as they might reasonably have done, the great danger of that long journey across the desert, infested with robber bands, but without delay they arranged a meeting that they might go together to comfort their distressed friend. Have all the friends who have so often and so freely ridiculed their words a record of equal faithfulness in regard to their own friends?

Then we further read that, when at last after their long and arduous journey they reached the place where Job lay, they were so moved by the condition in which they found him, and so truly made his sorrows their own, that they all three wept aloud and cast themselves down upon the ash-heap beside him. This is the spirit of true sympathy. How much it would do for the lightening of the heavy burdens of suffering humanity if the same spirit dwelt in the breast of every would-be comforter, if we were all willing to be so touched with the feeling of our

JOB'S LAMENT OF LIFE 91

fellows' infirmities, if we could all say with a sincere heart—

> "God's care be God's; 'tis mine to boast no joy
> Unsobered by such sorrows of my kind,
> As sully with their shade my light that shines."

In his first sermon after his wife's death, preached in the City Temple in a situation in which he could keenly appreciate the truth of these things, Dr Joseph Parker said—" The friends of Job entered into the genius of the occasion, which so few people can do. People want to make the occasion rather than accept it; hence the misery of what is called sympathy. Sometimes we do everything by doing nothing. Grief must have its time, and time is not a succession of moments; it is that and more. We make the moments, and thus we cruelly hurt ourselves by ticking off time into our pulses. Time is a great silent, flowing, gracious, all-healing river, and wherever the river cometh there is life." " ' My God, my God, why hast Thou forsaken me ? ' To some of us these words are a large portion of the New Testament. They create a great sanctuary of darkness where it is lawful to moan and to despair." Every one who has deep experience of life knows only too well that it contains such times as these.

So Job's friends sat down with him upon the ground seven days and seven nights, and none spake a word unto him; for they saw that his grief was very great. It is a great thing in a comforter if only he sees truly the greatness of the grief he seeks to heal. It is he who does not see the greatness of the grief, and therefore who does not feel the load of it, who will most readily allow his lips to overflow in shallow volubility. But a great grief can often best be ministered to by a great silence—a silence pregnant with that throbbing sympathy which is all the more deeply felt because it is not heard.

But the silence of Job's friends, although it was so rich in sympathy, was not therefore free from serious accusation; and it was exactly because this accusation was united to such sympathy that Job found it so terribly hard to bear. If these three men had been at enmity with him, or if they had been foolish and irreligious men, their opinions might have mattered little to the afflicted saint. But Job knew their great wisdom, he was familiar with their uprightness of character, they had often taken sweet counsel together, and he had always found them true as steel and faithful in their friendship to himself, even to the point of self-

JOB'S LAMENT OF LIFE

sacrifice, through the long, happy years that had now passed from him like a sunny dream.

These three men now looked upon their old friend with heart-breaking compassion; and yet they could not but acknowledge that their common creed condemned Job's life. And they felt all three, as even good men in such a case are so apt to do, that they must hold to their life-long creed, although it was so. Therefore they believed that the only explanation of their friend's calamities was that he had been guilty of some sin such as they had never dreamed could be connected with this outwardly noble and upright life—in other words, his sin had found him out.

Now although the three friends, with a fine sensitiveness which we cannot but admire, refrained for so long a period from expressing any of these thoughts, Job, with that piercing penetration of intense feeling, which such suffering as he was undergoing brings, read their thoughts in their faces as they sat day after day looking at him, and then looking at each other. And no doubt he divined their thoughts the more earnestly because their creed had until then been his own creed too, and because he felt that had any one of them fallen into his present situation he himself would have misjudged that man's case in the self-same way as they were misjudging his own.

This is the " fear " to which he refers in the end of his lament, and he found it to be great and terrible. " For the thing which I fear," he exclaimed, " cometh upon me, and that which I am afraid of cometh unto me. I am not at ease, neither am quiet, neither have I rest ; but trouble cometh." The longer they sat around him in silence, and the more sure he felt of the tenor of their thoughts towards him, the more insupportable that silence became to Job, until the long suppressed agony of his spirit, bitter as wounded love, and sorrowful as righteousness misunderstood, suddenly found utterance at last in the wild despairing cry with which the third chapter opens.

This, I think, is the true explanation of the very startling contrast between Job's attitude towards his calamities in the close of the second chapter and the wild thoughts which he utters in the third.

We have now reached the close of the prose prologue of the book. As we have seen even the prologue is rich in poetic conception and arrangement, but with the first speech of Job the work

JOB'S LAMENT OF LIFE   95

assumes the form of Hebrew poetry of the very highest order. We are made conscious of the change at once, even in the English translation, by the peculiar double movement or parallelism of expression, which is an essential characteristic of Hebrew poetry, and also by the exquisite beauty of the figures in which the deep thought is set forth.

Job begins his wild lament of life by cursing the day of his birth. He wishes all manner of evil to it, and curses also the preceding night as part of that day. He wishes that the very anniversary of that day may be doomed to sadness and to solitude. And in the vehemence of his emotion he calls upon all such as are skilful in the interpretation of evil omens to curse with him that day wherein he was born. All this is but a highly poetic expansion of the wish—Would that I had never been born.

At the eleventh verse the tragic fierceness of his passion is somewhat modified and the theme is changed into a plaintive hymn in praise of death. Job questions why, if he must be born, he did not die in his infancy and before he could be burdened with the conscious mystery and misery of life. He sings with a yearning melancholy, profoundly pathetic in such lips, of the peace and stillness of the grave, " Where the wicked cease from troubling, and where the weary are at rest "—where the great and the small, and the bond and the free, and even the good and the bad, are brought to one common level of unconscious inactivity.

At the twentieth verse there is again a change of theme, and Job, in a new access of agony and with exceeding boldness, proceeds to the arraignment of the providence of God. Why, he asks with a fierce rebelliousness of soul, why should he now be still kept alive, when life contains nothing for him but misery, when his future is dark with mystery, and when his very satisfaction of his simple bodily wants is accompanied with terrible pain.

His lament finds its climax in the expression of his conviction that the thing which he supremely feared is just about to be realised—that is to say, it has been borne in upon him during these last terrible days by the suggestive demeanour of his friends that they, even they who have known his life so long and so intimately, are about to interpret his calamity as the righteous judgment of God upon some hidden unrighteousness in his life, of which he knows himself to be innocent. It is this, above all, that forces him to utter that

JOB'S LAMENT OF LIFE 97

most pathetic wail, so full of tragic and heart-moving misery—" Wherefore is light given to him that is in misery, and life unto the bitter in soul; which long for death, and it cometh not; and dig for it more than for hid treasure; which rejoice exceedingly, and are glad when they can find the grave ? "

After we have read all this we feel that it can now no longer be said—" In all this did not Job sin with his lips." He has at last broken his great record. And wherein did the sin of Job's lament of life lie ? In answer to this question we may say that it lay first in its ingratitude to God. In the tempest of his soul Job has forgotten that life itself is a blessing. He has forgotten his own former argument which in a better frame of mind he used against the temptation of his wife—" What! Shall we receive good at the hand of God and shall we not receive evil ?" He shuts out from his consideration all the past joys of his life, which were the good gifts of the same God, against whose present providence his spirit rebels. And because he thus forgets what God has been to him he loses hope in any divine deliverance from his present bitter troubles. And how very common both this cause and consequence are in the lives of men ? How

G

frequently do men give way to the same desperate and despairing mood with far less reason than Job had ?

> " We overstate the ills of life and take
> Imagination, given us to bring down
> The choirs of singing angels, overshone
> By God's clear glory, down our earth to rake
> The dismal snows instead, flake following flake,
> To cover all the corn."

But Job's lament sinned further in its presumption. It is indeed an evil day for a man when he forgets the profound reverence which is due to God as his own Creator. It is well that we should sometimes ask ourselves the question—" Shall the thing formed say unto him that formed it, Why hast Thou made me thus ? " We have heard a great deal in modern times about the creature's claims upon his Creator. And there is no doubt comforting truth in that line of thought when it is wisely and rightly used. The creature has indeed some claims upon God simply by virtue of his being God's creature. But these claims are often strangely exaggerated, and oftener still they are misinterpreted altogether.

The child has claims upon the father. Yes, but of what nature are they ? Can the child rightly

JOB'S LAMENT OF LIFE 99

claim from the father that he should so gratify some foolish desire of his as to do his child a lasting wrong ? Is the child's claim that it should be answered by its father according to its own ignorance ? Is it not rather that it should be answered according to its father's wisdom and love ? Even so the claims of God's creatures upon Him may be truly summed up in this—that God, seeing that His wisdom is infinitely superior to that of His creatures, should therefore do, not what His creatures imagine, but what He knows to be for the highest good and the everlasting best of all His creatures, in view of all their relations to each other and to Himself. And who can judge of this but God alone ! Therefore there is no room for presumption, but much room for humility in our speaking of the providence of God.

Again, Job's lament sinned in its despair. This despair is deep and dark. We can scarcely see any resemblance in this first speech of Job to the noble and patient soul of the prologue. We look in vain for one ray of light in all his lament. It is as though his God had ceased to exist or had become his enemy. He wishes that he had never been born because the present troubles of his life are so great. Now there has indeed lived one man since then concerning whom it was said with supreme authority that it had been better for him if he had not been born. But observe that was so not because of any troubles in his life, but because of the magnitude of the sin which he would not be persuaded to forsake; and for no other reason could so terrible a thing be true of any son of man.

No man can ever have any reason for cursing God's precious gift of life to him, but many a man curses himself by his own abuse of that sacred gift. Nothing can be an abiding curse to any man but his own sin. Let him only forsake that and he has no reason to despair, for then will even the severest trials of life work out to his advantage; for " all things work together for good to them that love God "; but it is because men do not believe and act upon this great truth that the trials of life are so terrible to them as often to frustrate their highest uses.

> " O dreary life, we cry, O dreary life—
> And still the generations of the birds
> Sing through our sighing, and the flocks and herds
> Serenely live, while we are keeping strife
> With heaven's true purpose in us, as a knife
> Against which we may struggle."

JOB'S LAMENT OF LIFE

But although Job did indeed sin in uttering such wild and despairing words, yet we must not forget that there are things which must modify not a little our estimate of his sin. The first of these is the extreme character of his sufferings. These were so exceedingly great that they seem at times almost to have unhinged his mind. His words are sometimes not only wild and unreasonable, but even he himself acknowledges them to have been so when the terrible paroxysms of pain and passion are past and he has reached a calmer state. So in his answer to Eliphaz he refers to his own previous statements as—" The speeches of one that is desperate, which are as wind."

A second thing that ought to modify our estimate of Job's sin is the great darkness of the age in which he lived. There is clear enough evidence of this in the mythological references which occur even in the lament itself, as well as in other parts of the book. It would be utterly unjust to judge the utterances of Job when subjected to such suffering by the same standards by which the utterances of a Christian passing through a time of deep trial may be judged to-day ; for it is true here also that from him to whom much has been given shall much be required.

But lastly and chiefly we have God's own judgment upon the sin of Job set forth in the epilogue of the book to guide us in the formation of our own judgment in this respect. And when we consider that authoritative verdict we find that it is divinely considerate, rich in mercy, and full of a great compassion. There is nothing fragmentary or one-sided about it, but the conduct of Job is viewed as a whole. It is made plain, indeed, that Job had so sinned that there was an absolute necessity for his confession of his sin. But when God convinces Job of this there is nothing stinted about his confession, and so there is nothing stinted either about the divine forgiveness and the divine blessing.

What, then, is the answer to the bold questionings of Job which are nevertheless found at last to be better in God's sight than the smooth orthodoxy of his mistaken friends? The answer is not given by the friends of Job; but it is given by the great Friend of sinners. The answer is that death is not the solution nor the extinction of human troubles, but an incident—though a great and solemn one—in the progress of human life.

It is most remarkable that in all his discussion

JOB'S LAMENT OF LIFE 103

of his hopeless misery Job never once mentions suicide as a possible solution of the problem. That most miserable way out of the difficulty was left for such poor creatures as the hero of Matthew Arnold's greatest poem, "Empedocles on Etna," and for the central hope of the wretched philosophy of the German pessimist, Schopenhauer, who holds that this is the very worst of all possible worlds, inasmuch as if it were any worse than it actually is then, in his opinion, it could not continue to exist; so that to him the only dark deliverance conceivable consists in the weird nightmare of general suicide. But the writer of this great book of Job, however dim his vision of immortality of necessity was, knew so well that suicide is merely the delusion of one who is half coward and half madman that he does not think it worth while through all his great discussion even to mention it.

But the further Christian answer to the bold questionings of Job is that men are called to suffer that the work of God may be made manifest in them. We may not pretend to be able to comprehend the meaning of this great answer fully, and yet we may be able to see clearly enough the direction in which it leads — we may be able indeed to see this so clearly as to possess our souls in patience while we wait for the coming of further light, believing that this too will be vouchsafed to us in God's good time. This is the great wonder of innocent suffering, when a man suffers for God's sake, when a man's life becomes the theatre for the display of a divine glory which is often by no means apprehended until long after the display is past.

But further, a man may not only serve his God by his sufferings, he may very truly serve himself by these same sufferings too. Men suffer in order that they may be perfected in character and brought into a fuller knowledge of and into a closer communion with God. That is to say, they suffer for their own sakes as well as for God's sake, and these two ends of human suffering are not really separate from each other, but rather they coalesce into a deep unity in which the divine glory and the human good are one.

It is the vision of this high goal which, once clearly seen, makes all the affliction which may be steps to it seem light, and so, as Paul said— " Our light affliction, which is but for a moment, worketh for us a far more exceeding and eternal weight of glory, while we look, not at the things

JOB'S LAMENT OF LIFE 105

which are seen, but at the things which are not seen; for the things which are seen are temporal, but the things which are not seen are eternal." The cloud of suffering in the world is sometimes dark indeed, but it is in this way that the new light which Christ has brought into the world transforms it, as the departed sun transforms into masses of richly varied glory the great clouds of the west.

This, then, is what we supremely need—the light of Christ to work transformingly within the darkness of our lives. We need not so much new gifts, the divine meaning of which, by reason of our spiritual insensibility, we have no power to appreciate, but we do need gratitude, consecration, loving trust, that so the very trials and sorrows of life may be to us the shady places of sweet and solemn peace, where we may walk with God and learn, as with our weak hand in His, to value truly the blessings which we already have by becoming more worthy of them.

> " We cannot say the morning sun fulfils
> Ingloriously its course ; nor that the clear
> Strong stars, without significance, insphere
> Our habitation. We, meanwhile, our ills
> Heap up against this good : and lift a cry

Against this work-day world—this ill-spread feast,
As if ourselves were better certainly
Than what we come to. Maker and High-Priest,
I ask Thee not my joys to multiply,
Only to make me worthier of the least."

CHAPTER VI

THE ORTHODOX ARGUMENT AGAINST JOB

WE have seen in what way Job has been tried as well as comforted by the silence of his friends in the time of his great calamity, and in what wildly passionate language his suffering sensibility expressed itself. We are now to see how Job is to be further tried by the successive speeches of his friends, in which they more and more clearly formulate against him their accusations of that unrighteousness which his terrible troubles have established in their minds and of which they now feel that his wild, and to their minds impious speech, is corroborative evidence

After the three friends had listened to Job's terrible lament of life they felt, as they looked at each other with an expression of genuine religious horror, mingled with grief, that the time for silence was now past, and that something must be said, and said at once, in answer to such wild words. Job's, lament, therefore, forms the starting-point of the

108 AFFLICTIONS OF THE RIGHTEOUS

great debate. The debate consists of three circles of speeches in which each of the three friends is answered in turn by Job. But the increasing difficulty with which the friends maintain their position against the powerful arguments of Job is indicated not only by degeneration in their arguments, but also by the fact that in the third round Bildad is only able to contribute a few sentences in answer to Job's last speech. After Job has replied to these with crushing effect Zophar is unable to reply at all, and so the debate comes to a sudden collapse. Job is thus left master of the field, and concludes the whole discussion with a long speech of extraordinary power and beauty.

It is evident that to follow minutely the windings of this prolonged debate would carry us far beyond the scope of our present purpose. What I propose to do, therefore, is to treat the speeches on either side as a unity; and so in this chapter I will try to sum up the arguments of all the three friends as constituting the orthodox case against Job; and in the next chapter I will try to focus the arguments of Job in the same way in reply.

Viewing, then, the speeches of the friends in the general way indicated, there are two preliminary observations which we may make concerning them.

First, we should note their similarity. This reveals itself in the progress of the debate in three directions. In the first place, they are all alike in that they are expositions of the accepted orthodoxy of the day. It would have been easy for the writer of this great book to select for his characters men of widely differing religious views, representing the widely contrasted religions of different tribes and nations, if the book had been merely a poetic, and not also a historical composition.

But besides the evident probability that such a godly man as Job would have for his bosom friends just such orthodox and intelligent men as Eliphaz and Bildad and Zophar, no other kind of speakers would have so well suited the main purpose of the book. All the three friends are orthodox, and so in their three circles of speeches they have full opportunity to say all that can be said in defence of the doctrine which their position represents.

In the second place the speeches of the friends are similar in that they all move along the same three lines of rebuke and consolation and exhortation. These elements, as we shall see, are not present in equal proportions in each of the speeches, neither are they presented in the same order or with the same effect by each man, yet it is true of the speeches as a whole that they all move along these three main lines. In the third place the speeches are all alike in this, that they all show a marked increase of severity against Job as the debate proceeds. At first their sympathy with the sufferer is more in evidence, their rebukes are less stinging and cruel, and their exhortations are more mild and hopeful; but as the debate advances towards the close they all grow more and more fierce and merciless in their denunciations of what they regard as Job's impiety, and their sympathy for him gradually evaporates, until at last it practically reaches the vanishing point.

But while the speeches of the three men are in these three ways so similar, we should also note that the speeches of each have a well-marked individuality and originality of their own. Eliphaz, who speaks first, is evidently the eldest of the three, and his speeches are characterised by a mellowness of character and a ripeness of experience which we do not find in the speeches of his friends. He is also richer in sympathy towards Job than they, and the rebukes which he feels it necessary to administer to him are, especially at the beginning, more mild and considerate than those of the younger men.

ORTHODOX ARGUMENT AGAINST JOB 111

There is something touching in the conscious dilemma of the kindly old man between his deep pity for Job and his loyalty to orthodoxy, which is so beautifully expressed in the words with which he opens the debate. "If one assay to commune with thee," he asks, "wilt thou be grieved? But who can withhold himself from speaking?" He felt that Job had greatly erred in the passionate cries which he had uttered, and he did not believe that Job had any right to hold the opinions which prompted them. He felt, therefore, that his words must be rebuked; and yet to rebuke them faithfully was a most grievous task to his sympathetic nature, because he knew that such rebuke must add greatly to the distress of his already deeply afflicted friend. All this is characteristic of the attitude of Eliphaz towards Job, and of his method of conducting the argument.

The original characteristics of Bildad's contributions to the debate are penetration and hopefulness. He understands that there are states of mind into which men fall during seasons of great trial and periods of mental conflict and doubt in which pious observations and appeals to the divine authority of revelations vouchsafed to other men, such as Eliphaz had addressed to Job, have no weight with, and carry no conviction to the mind of the distracted and troubled one. With fine intuition Bildad perceives that Job's mind is at present in just this state of revolt. He therefore leaves the method of Eliphaz, and while he sometimes appeals to the general testimony of mankind in a rather wild and grandiloquent way, still he imports into his argument a new belief in the ultimate deliverance of Job calculated to be comfort indeed to the weary sufferer.

Bildad is himself a man of learning, richly versed in the lore of ancient times, and he sets himself to bring all the treasures of his learning to bear upon the mind of Job that he may be convinced of his error, and repent, and be saved. Yet in doing this he seeks to make it plain all the while that he is Job's true friend—that he sympathises with him deeply, and above all, that he still hopes and believes the best for him; and the remarkably bright words which he uses in his earlier arguments show not only how fervent was his desire for the good of his friend, but also how strong was his faith that the actual issue would indeed be even as he desired.

" Behold," he declares, " God will not cast away a perfect man, neither will He uphold the evil-doers.

He will yet fill thy mouth with laughter, and thy lips with shouting." Bildad's penetrating and hopeful mind gets glimpses of the truth that, notwithstanding his creed, and nothwitstanding Job's condition, and in the absence of any stronger proof than imaginations to the contrary, Job's claim to integrity, which was so powerfully supported by his whole life, could not be denied. He *is* a perfect man, and if so, God will surely awake for him and bless him.

When we turn to the speeches of Zophar we miss both the sympathy and experience of Eliphaz and the penetration and hopefulness of Bildad. We find Zophar's speeches, too, have a character all their own. Not only from the fact that he speaks last and is the first to break down in argument, but also from the characteristic features of his speeches, we shall probably be right if we suppose that he was the youngest of Job's three friends. He makes no attempt to put himself in Job's place, or to imagine how cruel from such a view-point must the theology appear which he so rudely tries to thrust upon Job. Rather he carries on the debate with a new fierceness, with a hot-headed zeal which lacks knowledge, with a self-confidence which does not lack presumption, and with an insolent intolerance which suggests a bad temper rather than a worthy indignation.

Job's arguments seemed utter blasphemy to such a man as Zophar. It appeared to him that if such ideas as Job expressed were to be endured, the very foundations of religion would be destroyed. He had received it as a tradition from his forefathers that the moral government of the world was carried forward on principles that were radically opposed to such ideas, and his mind was too narrow and his views of life too stereotyped to enable him to enter into an impartial consideration of the new suggestions which the speeches of Job had raised. He held that his theology was incapable of improvement, and that any theory of Providence which opposed itself to the theory which he had inherited could only be a wild and impious heresy.

He was quite a sincere man, but that did not prevent him from being a deplorably bigoted, and even in some respects an unjust one. For as we often see, especially in connection with religious controversy, a man who freely allows himself to get very angry with any one who ventures to make any statement which does not exactly square with his particular theories is precisely the very man who holds himself at liberty to attack the sincere

ORTHODOX ARGUMENT AGAINST JOB 115

opinions of others who happen to differ from him, and that, too, with most unnecessary heat and quite uncharitable bitterness. "Should a man full of talk be justified? Should thy boastings make men hold their peace? And when thou mockest, shall no man make thee ashamed?" This is how Zophar proceeds at once in his first speech to plunge the knife of his inconsiderate and unfair argument into the heart of the suffering Job.

He endeavours to represent Job as a babbling, boastful fool, a vain wind-bag, who had nothing better to support his novel and impious position than the length of time he could continue to pour forth empty talk about it. Now this was not only harsh and insolent, but it was also radically false and unjust. Undoubtedly Job in his intense and passionate speeches had uttered words which were open to legitimate criticism. He had been made to feel very keenly that his friends were endeavouring to fit the round pin of their traditional theology into the square hole of his troubled life, and that it left the whole four corners of his experience unaccounted for, and in his passionate resentment at this treatment he had spoken words which he himself in calmer moments afterwards was most willing to withdraw.

If Zophar had directed Job's attention to these sayings of his in a spirit which blended together earnest faithfulness to the truth as he knew it, with true sympathy for the afflicted man, and with a charitable consideration of the terrible circumstances in which Job spoke, then he would have been acting worthily the part of a true friend. But Zophar not only treated the defects of Job's speeches with an insolent intolerance, but he ignored their many great virtues and utterly misrepresented their general tone and spirit. No wonder, therefore, that it was Zophar who stung Job into the biting satire—" No doubt but ye are the men, and wisdom will die with you." Whatever may be said of Job's speeches, they are just as far as possible from being the utterances of a long-winded babbler.

The second of the two speeches of Zophar is wholly occupied with picturing in an abstract way the terribleness of the divine judgment upon the wicked man. It is either wholly irrevelant or it is the most cruel of all the speeches against Job, and we seem forced to accept the latter alternative. The speeches of all the three friends are not without either earnestness or ability, but in respect to both of these high qualities they fall far below the

ORTHODOX ARGUMENT AGAINST JOB 117

exalted level of the speeches of Job, and undoubtedly the deliverances of Zophar are furthest of all behind.

Now the argument of the three friends against Job, taken as a whole, may be comprehensively summed up in six propositions, each alternative proposition being a deduction of the one that immediately precedes it. In this way :—

I. The first proposition asserts the infinite greatness of God in wisdom and power in contrast with the littleness of man in his weakness and ignorance.

II. The second proposition, which is a deduction from the first, asserts that it is impious presumption for man, and so for Job in particular, to attempt to criticise the providence of God.

III. The third proposition asserts that God, being absolutely just, and having no motive to be unjust, deals perfect justice to every man, both the good and the bad, in this world.

IV. The fourth proposition, which is a deduction from the third, asserts that every man's experience reveals his true character, in prosperity his righteousness, in adversity his wickedness. Therefore Job is very wicked.

V. The fifth proposition asserts that God chastises good men for the evil in them in order that they may be perfected.

VI. The sixth and last proposition, which is a deduction from the fifth, asserts that if the good man who has sinned confesses and repents, God will certainly forgive him and restore him to prosperity. That, therefore, is the one hope for Job.

This, then, being the structure of the argument against Job considered as a whole, it will be most convenient for us to consider these propositions in successive pairs.

The first pair deals with God's greatness in contrast with man's littleness, and the consequent presumption in any man's attempt to criticise the providence of God. Each of the three friends in turn speak of the greatness and incomprehensibility of God as a sufficient reason why Job should be humble before Him, and cease to revolt against His providence as he does. Eliphaz says—" As for me I would seek unto God, and unto God I would commit my cause : Which doeth great

ORTHODOX ARGUMENT AGAINST JOB 119

things and unsearchable ; marvellous things without number : Who giveth rain upon the earth, and sendeth waters upon the fields : so that He setteth up on high those that be low ; and those which mourn are exalted to safety. He frustrateth the devices of the crafty, that so their hands cannot perform their enterprise. He taketh the wise in their own craftiness ; and the counsel of the froward is carried headlong." " Is not God in the height of heaven ? " he asks again, " And behold the height of the stars, how high they are ! And thou sayest, What doth God know ? Can He judge through the thick darkness ? "

He suggests to Job that the humble contemplation of God's wisdom and power as exhibited in His works should beget that deep reverence towards the divine Being without which real religion is impossible—that these works are there not for their own sakes, but chiefly that they may reveal God and so commend him to man as to win His trust and adoration. But as we often see, the very contemplation of God's incomprehensible greatness sometimes drives the proud soul into revolt, just because it is proud and impatient of its own limitations.

120 AFFLICTIONS OF THE RIGHTEOUS

"How summer bright are yonder skies,
And earth as fair in hue;
And yet what sign of ought that lies
Behind the green and blue?

But man to-day is Fancy's fool,
As man hath ever been;
The nameless Power or Powers that rule,
Were never heard or seen."

That is David Hume made melodious by Alfred Tennyson. That is the confusion of sublime Faith with foolish Fancy. It is the poet's representation of a sad, proud soul that has become rebellious in its pride. And yet it is a remarkable fact that the same contemplation will lead a meek and humble soul to deeper humility and a calmer happier rest in God, so that he will even make it a ground of praise that he can say—"O the depth of the riches both of the wisdom and knowledge of God! How unsearchable are His judgments and His ways past finding out; for who hath known the mind of the Lord? or who hath first given Him and it shall be recompensed unto him again? For of Him and through Him and to Him are all things; to Whom be glory forever. Amen."

When such minds consider the works of God they are not only impressed by their mystery and

ORTHODOX ARGUMENT AGAINST JOB 121

incomprehensibility, but they are enraptured by the power and wisdom, and, most of all, by the benevolence which they display. And indeed, the man who cannot see at least something of this lavish goodness and benevolence of God in all the manifold arrangements around him and above him and beneath him, in the produce of the earth, in the wonderful and varied mineral stores of the earth, in the systematic and unbroken procession of the seasons, in the cleansing and reviving ministry of the winds, in the unfailing bestowal of necessary dews and rains, in the marvellous periodic heavings and swellings and windings of the great ocean tides and currents, and in the complex relative movements of sun and moon and stars, the slightest derangement or failure of whose majestic motions would produce the most appalling catastrophes which the imagination of man can picture forth—the man who can consider these things and yet fail to discern in them the abounding proofs, not only of divine power and wisdom, but also of divine benevolence, is not only blind but culpably blind, and is the last being on the face of the earth who should attempt to pass any judgment upon the wonderful providence of God.

Sometimes the argument from God's greatness

is presented by the friends in a crude form, as if the mere magnitude of the divine power alone were a sufficient basis for moral conclusions, as when Bildad says—" Dominion and fear are with Him ; He maketh peace in His high places. Is there any number of His armies ? And upon whom doth not His light arise ? How then can man be just with God," where the inconsequence of the deduction comes upon us with a kind of moral shock.

And as Bildad tries to overawe Job by the vision of omnipotence, so Zophar endeavours to humble him by an impressive consideration of the omniscience of God in contrast to the ignorance of man. " Oh, that God would speak," he exclaims, " and open His lips against thee ; and that He would show thee the secrets of wisdom, that it is manifold in effectual working ! Know, therefore, that God exacteth of thee less than thine iniquity deserveth. Canst thou by searching find out God ? Canst thou find out the Almighty to perfection ? It is high as heaven ; what canst thou do ? Deeper than Sheol ; what canst thou know ? The measure thereof is longer than the earth. If He pass through, and shut up, and call unto judgment, then who can hinder Him ? "

ORTHODOX ARGUMENT AGAINST JOB 123

Here the language is most impressive, but the argument is weak and unconvincing because of the same moral inconsequence. It is the imposing declaration of what is indeed a great truth, and one of which men often need to be reminded—that the problems of life can never be to God what they are to us, that He knows us better than we know ourselves, all our weaknesses and all our sins; and also that it is quite vain for us to imagine that we can so understand Him that we can be fit to judge His ways with men. Our judgment of the divine Providence must ever be imperfect because our knowledge is imperfect. We cannot know God as He knows Himself. Many of His purposes are doubtless too great and many-sided for us to comprehend. God alone is His own interpreter.

Men are often still made to feel what the psalmist felt when they seek to form for themselves a reasoned out account of the more mysterious facts and experiences of life—" Such knowledge is too high for me, I cannot attain unto it." But both Bildad and Zophar present the argument in such a way that in regard to Job's case it is somewhat beside the point. Job never dreamed that by searching he could find out God. He was profoundly conscious of his own inferiority to Him. What his whole soul hungered for was some adequate explanation of God's apparent injustice towards himself, some real reconciliation of the moral contradictions of the divine Providence as he felt them in his own experience.

The way in which Eliphaz handles the argument from God's greatness comes nearer to meeting this need than the way in which it is used by Bildad and Zophar. Eliphaz argues that Job's revolt against God's providence is unreasonable, simply because there is none to whom he can appeal beyond God. " Call now, he says, Is there any that will answer thee ? And to which of the holy ones wilt thou turn ? "

This may not be all that the shattered nerves, quivering under some strong agony, require. There may be some further answer required to calm the terrible unrest of the questioning soul which is distracted to the point of madness by the bitter mysteries of life, mysteries which are so intolerably hard to bear for this very reason above all others, that they seem to represent man as forsaken of God, nay, smitten of God and afflicted, when he is most earnestly striving to do His will. And yet the fact that there is no appeal from God,

ORTHODOX ARGUMENT AGAINST JOB

no help beyond Him, or apart from Him, is a great fact, which must be seriously reckoned with. To whom can we go but unto Him? And it is something gained if a man is even constrained to approach God as a forlorn hope and commit his case to Him, even in this unworthy way; for it is the glory of God that He is so very different from man, that even such a man coming to Him in such a way He will in no wise cast out. If a man will only submit to and confide in God he will soon begin to understand God better, and instead of being his forlorn hope God will soon become his supreme joy.

But, as Eliphaz further suggests to Job, revolt against God's providence is proved to be unreasonable, even by the effects which it produces upon the man who so revolts. Wrath against God is a man's own deadly foe, and is therefore foolish in the extreme. " For wrath killeth the foolish man, and indignation slayeth the silly one." Such wrath of man worketh not the righteousness of God, but often the man's own ruin. This argument has real force against many of the utterances of Job, although it does not apply in the way nor to the extent that Eliphaz supposed.

The second pair of propositions which go to make up the orthodox case against Job deal with the absolute justice of God and the consequence of that, namely, that every man's experience in this world is the revelation of his character, in prosperity of his righteousness, and in adversity of his wickedness. Job's great adversity, therefore, argues great wickedness in him.

Eliphaz states the argument concisely in his challenge—" Is not thy fear of God thy confidence, and thy hope the integrity of thy ways ? Remember, I pray thee, who ever perished being innocent, and where were the righteous cut off ? " This challenge is evidently based upon the orthodox position that prosperity is the divine seal of goodness, and vice versa. The doctrine is fully formulated in the passage that follows it. It is an argument to which the three friends return again and again in different forms.

The steps of it may be stated thus—First, a righteous man is prosperous and cannot perish. If such a man be in temporary trouble he is to fall back upon his own conscious goodness, and in relation thereto the certain justice of God—" He shall certainly be delivered." " Who ever perished

ORTHODOX ARGUMENT AGAINST JOB 127

being innocent?" Secondly, the unrighteous are unprosperous and do perish. "By the breath of God they perish, and by the blast of his anger are they consumed." Lastly, when a seemingly good man suffers even to hopelessness and is reduced to incurable ruin, then it is plain that he is not really the man that men had thought him, he is an unmasked hypocrite; for—" Shall mortal man be more just than God? Shall a man be more pure than his Maker?"

Now this is just where the pinch of the false theory grips the suffering Job; for according to this argument the very severity of his calamity is the thing that seals his hopeless condemnation. Thus he is made to appear as " one condemned by heaven, an outcast from his God." Eliphaz feels more deeply than his two friends the greatness of this difficulty, and bends all his strength to meet it. But in the end he is driven to the same refuge as they. God must be true and every man a liar—Job must be bad that God may still be good.

Bildad handles the same argument with less considerateness. " How long shall the words of thy mouth be like a mighty wind?" he demands of Job. " Doth God pervert judgment? Or doth the Almighty pervert justice?" To the mind of Bildad that was really the only alternative if the theory which he and his friends held so tenaciously was to be rejected. Their position simply amounted to this—We must be right or God must be wrong. They persistently assumed that there could only be these two alternatives, and they sought to force Job to accept the first by pressing home upon his religious consciousness the appalling nature of the second.

This is a line of argument that is often taken by well-meaning orthodox people to-day; and, in fact, it has been too common in every generation. People who have received their religious beliefs as a kind of mental and spiritual legacy from those who have gone before them, and who have never examined them and tested them for themselves to see if they can really be to them what they were to their fathers—such people have simply no idea of the necessary progress of spiritual knowledge, and the consequent readjustments of faith. And they are not only unthankful for, but also most intolerant of, the laborious strivings of earnest living minds after the achievement of such progress —strivings which alone redeem them and the majority of their fellows from spiritual stagnation, and which are the rising rays upon the general gloom that prophesy the coming of a fairer, fuller day.

Such people simply do not know what serious soul-struggle after the personal acquisition of the truth means. Other souls have struggled and reached conclusions in which they found peace. And lo! these who have come after them, without any struggle, but with a most unworthy spiritual sloth, seek to steal these doctrines, which were attained as with bloody sweat, and to make these, the true meaning of which they cannot possibly know, the final conclusions for themselves and for their contemporaries about God's methods of government for the individual and for the race; and so they behave as if they had nothing to learn in these high matters of supreme importance.

It was a pitiful fruit of Bildad's false theology which forced him to put the very worst construction possible upon the dreadful calamity which had befallen Job's children, and then to use that as an argument to their father in order to get him to subscribe to the same theology when it was crushing with insupportable severity against himself. Bildad feels that there is a moral necessity for God's punishing the wicked on the one hand, and for His blessing the righteous on the other. Where he errs is in limiting both the time and the method of these divine awards ; for he has no other thought than that they must be given within the circle of this little life, and that the marks of God's anger must be sorrow and calamity, and the proof of His approval must be temporal advancement and prosperity.

Zophar's contribution to this part of the argument is characteristic. In his profound and searching arguments Job had stated a great many undeniable facts which overturned the false theory of Providence which all his three friends embraced, and which they made the basis of their condemnation of his life. The chief business of Zophar in following in the debate was to examine these facts and either to disprove their validity, or, having accepted them, to show how they could be made to square with the theory of Providence which he maintained. But Zophar did neither of these things. What he did was to shut his eyes close against these unwelcome facts, and to embark upon a vehement denunciation of the conclusions drawn from them. But to ignore an argument is not the same thing as to answer it.

Zophar shows plainly enough that he is incapable of truly appreciating the arguments of Job, with which he does not attempt to deal. He is unable to distinguish between Job's earnest expostulation with God and the irreverent infidelity that mocks Him, and he confuses Job's claim of integrity and sincerity with a declaration of purity of doctrine and absolute personal innocence. The great problem of justification as it presented itself to the mind of Job had not yet even begun to dawn upon the mind of Zophar. Because he shut out all the inconvenient facts which did not harmonise with his hereditary creed he did not see any difficulty in continuing to hold that creed; and, moreover, he was disposed to be very impatient with any man whose moral and spiritual vision was clearer and more penetrating than his own. It was this blindness, this easy self-satisfaction and incapacity to do justice to life's deeper questions on the part of his friends, which made Job feel that intense desire which he again and again expressed to get past these false apologists for God that he might deal with God Himself.

Characteristically Zophar thinks that if God did speak He would be certain to speak against Job and in favour of himself. He does not in the least seem to perceive that his hard argument that Job, notwithstanding the severity of his sufferings, is after all suffering less than he deserves to suffer, has a double edge, and sets himself in an almost ludicrous light of unmeasured self-complacency. For if Job ought to suffer more than all this physical and mental agony to which he is being subjected, then what manner of man must Zophar be in comparison to Job, he for whom God has appointed no pain nor suffering, but whom He continues to bless with much prosperity! There is undoubtedly a deep truth in this observation of Zophar; but God is no respecter of persons, and therefore it is of general application. As Shakespeare has it—" Use every man after his desert, and who should 'scape whipping?" Certainly not the Zophars among men.

Now no theory of Providence which has been held by multitudes of men for ages, even although it has many errors, can be wholly destitute of truth. And the great truth which was the strength of this false theory so distressing to Job was that it conceived of God as ceaselessly working for righteousness in the government of the world. With all their defects we see that the goodness

ORTHODOX ARGUMENT AGAINST JOB 133

of God's character is the supreme consideration in the minds of Job's friends. The perfect righteousness of God is distinctly first in their thoughts. That is a great truth and a noble aim, however wrongly it may be argued for. It is great enough to save from contempt any theory of Providence of which it forms a part. And it is for ever the one sufficient consolation to distressed saints in times when wickedness both triumphs and abounds.

But then this beautifully rounded theory, like so many others, most grievously erred in the limitations which it presumptuously imposed on the eternal God in His dealings with His creatures. No doubt some excuse is to be found for this in the extreme dimness of the hope of immortality men had in that far back age, and which is plainly evidenced in these speeches. And yet enough had already been revealed to make this false interpretation of Providence blameworthy, as we see from the divine verdict in the epilogue.

If the three friends had said that God would find a way which they themselves could not yet discern to justify and reward the righteous, whatever sufferings might overwhelm them, then they would have continued to show faith in the justice of God, and at the same time they would have shown faith in the goodness of man. But, like many other men to-day, they were too anxious to explain what they could not explain. They suffered their vision to be blocked by the tombstone. They thought it necessary that a poetic justice should be realised within the narrow limits of this little life, and so they cruelly denounced their friend.

There are still many who grudge God time for the execution of His purposes. They forget what are the years of the Most High. Men are still very apt to fall into the attitude of mind which Christ's disciples fell into after His death and before they knew of His resurrection—namely, that death closes the possibilities of a life, and that the justification and interpretation of it is to be looked for rather from all that took place before death than from anything that can happen after it.

Now how great a saint Job was appears from the fact that he rose to a far higher attitude of mind than this in relation to the mysteries of God's providence, notwithstanding the terrible position in which he found himself. Job lived in the days of abounding mystery, when the hope of a life beyond the grave was so dim as to be even very doubtful to most minds; and yet through his very sufferings his faith gathered such a splendid strength as to pierce through the surrounding gloom to God's unclouded light, and to express itself in those glorious words, by which we still express even our Christian faith in its moments of most triumphant anticipation—" I know that my Redeemer liveth, and that He shall stand at the latter day upon the earth: and that after my skin hath been thus destroyed, yet in my flesh shall I see God : Whom I shall see for myself and mine eyes shall behold, and not another; though my reins be consumed within me."

In the third pair of propositions, which conclude the orthodox argument against Job, the three friends set forth a theory of the divine correction according to which God chastises good men in order to purge them from the remaining evil in them, and this is applied hypothetically and more or less doubtfully by all the three friends to the case of Job. It is only along this line that they offer him any real comfort; but we are to observe that it is always offered to him on a condition that he cannot conscientiously accept, namely, that he should confess himself guilty of great and extraordinary sins in order to justify

God for inflicting upon him such extraordinary calamities.

"Behold," says Eliphaz, "happy is the man whom God correcteth, therefore despise not thou the chastening of the Almighty." This is often a needed warning, for God's chastisements are being every day despised, when trouble is regarded as a mere accident, when men refuse to see the hand of God in their affliction, and when the high moral purpose of some severe trial is heedlessly or stubbornly ignored. But the speeches of Job abundantly prove that it was far otherwise with him.

Eliphaz urges Job to receive the divine correction meekly by reminding him that God heals as well as wounds. He further seeks to strengthen his exhortation by promising that to the man who receives divine correction humbly God will add temporal prosperity to deliverance. The very stones of the fields will be in league with him in the production of a plenteous harvest. His flocks and possessions shall be unharmed by wild beasts. His household shall prosper in peace. He himself shall die full of years and honour, and his numerous children shall succeed like himself, for he shall not die until he has seen them also become great.

ORTHODOX ARGUMENT AGAINST JOB 137

Bildad's argument takes the same line. He says to Job—"If thou wouldst seek diligently unto God, and make thy supplication to the Almighty; if thou wert pure and upright, surely now He would awake for thee." Job had said— "*If* I have sinned." That is, if he had sinned in such an extraordinary way as to account for his extraordinary sufferings. But Bildad finds the conclusive proof that Job had so sinned in his present condition, and so he says that if Job will confess that, and repent that, God will hear him and will so bless him that the beginning of his career, with all its greatness, will appear but small in comparison with its splendid end. Bildad's picture of that end quite rivals that of Eliphaz in its ideal rosy colourings. The prosperity of the wicked man, he says, is frail and transient as a spider's web, but the prosperity of the righteous is great and abiding.

But what bearing has all this upon the case of Job, unless he should grant, what he most earnestly denies, that he is to be classed as specially wicked, that his past prosperity was that of a secretly wicked man, and that he now suffers more than his hortatory friends because he has been more wicked than they? Job, too, is ready to acknow-

138 AFFLICTIONS OF THE RIGHTEOUS

ledge that there are those who are wicked as well as those who are righteous in the world, and that God is with the latter and against the former. But the great question is—Who are the wicked, and who are the righteous ? By what are they to be distinguished and revealed ? Is the dark brand of suffering and of sorrow the supreme criterion by which this great division is to be made ? So Job's friends persistently assert. But against this Job, in his conscious integrity, utterly revolts ; nay, the bare idea that it might be so fills him with an agony of doubt and shakes his faith in the goodness and the faithfulness of God. And we know that Job was right and that his friends were wrong ; for otherwise not only would all the prophets and martyrs who suffered and died for the truth be ranged among the enemies of God, but Christ Himself would be distinguished as the most wicked of men.

In his prosecution of the same argument the reformation which Zophar demands of Job as the condition of his deliverance is very thorough and comprehensive. First he must set his heart right : he must bring himself into a right state of thought and feeling towards God. Next, he must pray, seeking from God not what his iniquity deserves, but

ORTHODOX ARGUMENT AGAINST JOB 139

what God's mercy may bestow. This he must follow by a practical reformation of his conduct—although Zophar, like the other two advisers of Job, cannot point out wherein that conduct had been wrong. Finally he must see that his home is purged from all unrighteousness, lest another dreadful judgment of God should fall upon it. "If thou set thine heart aright," he says, "and stretch out thine hands toward Him; if iniquity be in thine hand, put it far away, and let not unrighteousness dwell in thy tents; surely, then, shalt thou lift up thy face without spot; yea, thou shalt be steadfast and shalt not fear." The great Greek poet, Aeschylus, has most truly said :—

> "How easy when the foot is not entangled
> In misery's thorny maze, to give monitions
> And precepts to the afflicted!"

Zophar strikingly illustrates this truth. Job had made sincere endeavours in the directions indicated by Zophar. It is the man who has done so who knows best that if he regards iniquity in his heart the Lord will not hear him. It is he who feels that the perfect guidance of life is from God alone and is ever ready to cry—" Search me, O God, and know my heart; try me and know my thoughts; and see if there be any wicked way in me, and lead me in the way everlasting." That was the real attitude of Job's mind, although his words were sometimes so wild that they could not be justified.

The divine reward which Zophar promises as the result of the reformation which he urges is expressed with great poetic beauty. God will cause Job's trouble to pass away into the region of forgetfulness, and the very memory of it shall only be like the waters of a stream that have long since flowed past. His future life shall be like the glorious dawn, in which if there is any darkness it shall speedily disappear. It shall be as the path of the just that shineth more and more unto the perfect day. His days shall be arched with a divine rainbow of new hope, and be full of a new security and peace.

But the deepest and the most mysterious element in Job's agony was just the contrast which his present experience presented, notwithstanding his conscious integrity, to all such glowing pictures as these. Job needed greater words than any of his friends could speak—words which Christ alone could speak. We need not blame them because they could not say more, yet they deserve blame

ORTHODOX ARGUMENT AGAINST JOB 141

because they did not say less. They had no right to be so sure that all the light that they could give was enough for Job's deep need, and that God had nothing better to say than they had. They were fond of reminding Job that God did "great things and unsearchable." There they were right. But they went on to say of some of the deepest mysteries of His providence—"Lo! this, *we* have searched it." There they were utterly wrong.

It is often so. God's providence is all right; but it is often quite beyond our understanding, and it is our over-confident interpretation of it that is wrong, and that sometimes so monstrously misrepresents God. It is true that Light has come into the world; but it is often still true also that the darkness comprehendeth it not. We need purer vision and larger powers in order that we may fully appreciate and use that "light of the knowledge of the glory of God" that shines from the face of Jesus Christ. As Tennyson beautifully says in his "Ancient Sage":—

> "My son, the world is dark with griefs and graves,
> So dark that men cry out against the Heavens.
> Who knows but that the darkness is in man?
> The doors of Night may be the gates of Light;
> For were thou born or blind or deaf, and then
> Suddenly heal'd, how would'st thou glory in all

AFFLICTIONS OF THE RIGHTEOUS

The splendours and the voices of the world !
And we, the poor earth's dying race, and yet
No phantoms, watching from a phantom shore,
Await the last and largest sense to make
The phantom walls of this illusion fade,
And show us that the world is wholly fair."

CHAPTER VII

JOB'S REPLY TO HIS FRIENDS

HAVING stated and examined the orthodox argument of the three friends against Job we have now to consider the very unorthodox argument by which Job in his successive speeches replies to them. In these speeches of Job the Hebrew poet exerts the full power of his genius, and in them both the thought and the expression of the thought sometimes reach an amazing height of poetic beauty and philosophic power. The poet evidently intends a contrast between the calm and logical theorising of the friends, who are at their ease, and the passionate, erratic intensity of the suffering Job. The mind of Job all through the debate is seen to be in a state of tumult, due to his terrible condition, and although at some times he is less violently agitated than at others he is always in a state of deep unrest. His argument, therefore, is everywhere broken up by cries of physical and mental agony, by outbursts of denunciation against his friends, by bold expostulations with God, and by wails of self-pity or appeals for sympathy which often reach a wonderful depth of pathos.

Notwithstanding all this, however, these speeches of Job, when we carefully consider them as a whole, disclose to us a profound scheme of thought on the great subjects under discussion which is none the less convincing because it is presented with the irregularity natural to the deep and sometimes even wild tides of emotion to which Job was so helplessly exposed.

To begin with there is one division in his thought which is so well marked that none can fail to note it. That is, that while a great portion of his speeches is occupied with controverting the arguments of his friends, another very considerable portion is taken up with a series of remarkable expostulations which are addressed directly to God Himself. This is so clear and so significant a division that it will be best for us to deal in this chapter only with Job's argument against his friends, reserving for the next our consideration of his expostulations with God.

Job opens his argument against his friends in answer to the first speech of Eliphaz by a strong complaint on the way in which they are conducting the case against him. He often repeats this com-

JOB'S REPLY TO HIS FRIENDS 145

plaint, and more and more vehemently as the debate goes on. It always proceeds along two main lines : he reproaches them for their lack of human sympathy and considerateness, because they do not make sufficient allowance for the terrible condition in which they see him ; and he accuses them of steadily endeavouring to make the worst instead of seeking to make the best of his case, and therefore he complains that they are unjust both to himself and to God.

With his very first words Job shows that his mind is open to fair and reasonable correction, for he opens his defence with an apology for the rash words he had used in his lament of life ; but even his apology is touched with the spirit of anguish, and throbs with the irrepressible complaint of his self-pity. " O that my vexation were but weighed," he exclaims, " and my calamity laid in the balances together. For now it would be heavier than the sand of the seas. Therefore have my words been rash." Job acknowledges that he has been impatient and has spoken rashly, but he excuses himself by the greatness of his sufferings. He keenly feels the want of the adequate appreciation of these sufferings by his friends. He is sure that if they but knew these

K

as he does, they would view his whole case very differently, and speak very differently too.

Job often expresses this thought in different forms, and his words are sometimes like the great sighs of a breaking heart that is utterly misunderstood by its dearest friends. They are the expression of an intense longing for a fair hearing and a true judgment, which he sees no hope of obtaining. He knows that he is being deeply wronged by those whose opinion he most values, but how to prove it so he cannot find. Job illustrates his argument by the behaviour of the lower animals. "Doth the wild ass bray when he hath grass, or loweth the ox over his fodder?" There is a suggestion here that his friends have fodder. They have no reason to utter cries of anguish or complaint. They are at ease and possessed of every comfort. Their's has been a one-sided experience of life. As for Job he has known both life's brightness and its darkness. He did not always cry as he does now His words also were once as smooth as his theories. He never knew that that view of Providence was so poor and shallow and insufficient until knowledge entered into him by suffering. He is now further on than his old friends in the true ascension of the soul, for he is moving up rapidly toward perfection

JOB'S REPLY TO HIS FRIENDS 147

through his suffering, though it be with many wild cries of bodily pain and of far deeper soul agony.

Job believed himself to be dying. Now it is a trial of fearful severity for a good man in his last days to have his whole life misunderstood and misjudged by his dearest friends in regard to those things that have ever been most precious to him. Hence the bitterness of Job's complaint. "To him that is ready to faint," he says, " kindness should be showed by his friend : even to him that forsaketh the fear of the Almighty." He felt that even if he had been the kind of man they thought him they should still have dealt more tenderly and considerately with him. If his faith had failed towards God that was no reason why their sympathetic faithfulness should fail towards him.

This reproach Job expands figuratively with equal force and beauty, and with such detail as to show how acutely he was suffering from the treatment of his friends. He says—" My brethren have dealt deceitfully as a brook." With graphic power he pictures the weary and thirsty caravans toiling through the desert in their seven days' journey from Tema, or their still longer journey from Sheba, under the blazing sun. They turn aside to seek refreshment where the brook used to flow, but it is only to be bitterly disappointed and confounded when they find that the very heat which made them need it so much has dried up its waters, and that its channels are dry as the arid desert sands, So, says Job, looking with deep reproach upon his friends, " Now ye are nothing ; ye see a terror and are afraid." The very heat of Job's affliction, which made his need of their tender comfort so great, was the very thing which dried up their faith in his integrity. They looked upon him as a terror—a man who was evidently set forth as an object lesson of divine judgment, and so they were afraid to be too kind to him, lest they also should come under the same condemnation.

Job reminds them how little he had asked from them, not to risk their life, not even to part with any of their property for his sake. He asked not their substance but their sympathy. He asked not for cold and logical theorising founded upon unfair speculation as to the secrets of his life, but for upright and straightforward argument which did not evade nor distort the facts. " How forcible are words of uprightness," he exclaims, " but what doth your arguing reprove ? " He feels that they have caught at and made the

JOB'S REPLY TO HIS FRIENDS 149

worst of the wild and desperate words that had been wrung from him in the paroxysms of his pain. He is moved to indignation as he thinks of this, and declares that they are allowing themselves to be governed by a spirit that would cast lots for an orphan and make merchandise of a friend. He demands a new method in their judgment of his case, not lofty censoriousness, not even compassion, but simple justice. "Return, I pray you, let there be no injustice; yea, return again, my cause is righteous."

The next stage in Job's presentation of his case is the manner in which he deals with the argument of his friends concerning the infinite greatness of God and the consequent impiety of any man presuming to criticise His Providence. As we have seen, this is a very favourite argument with the friends, and as they constantly recur to it Job has to deal with it again and again in the progress of the debate. And the way in which he deals with it is this. In the first place, he shows how entirely he is in agreement with them in regard to all, and far more than all, that they say about the greatness of God, both with respect to His wisdom and His power. But notwithstanding this full admission his friends come back to the subject again and again, until at last Job gets exasperated and complains that they address him in regard to this matter as if he were an ignoramus, and reminds them that he is not destitute of brains. They continually try to silence him by long descriptions of the power and wisdom of God. But who, cries Job, does not know that the power and wisdom of God are incomparable ? Why, he exclaims, the very beasts and birds and fish might teach such truths, the evidence of which abounds on every hand.

Their persistence in this line of argument leads Job himself to paint such pictures of the divine wisdom and power that they far excel those of his friends. He deals with the subject in a comprehensive and penetrating manner, bringing out unwelcome facts which they did not see, and did not wish to see, and showing that the ways in which God sometimes used his wisdom and power in the world did not support, but rather utterly destroyed their mechanical theory of God's moral government with regard to rewards and punishments. After having done this he says with crushing effect—" Lo ! mine eye hath seen all this, mine ear hath heard and understood it. What ye know the same do I know also : I am not inferior to you." And everyone who reads Job's

JOB'S REPLY TO HIS FRIENDS 151

words with understanding will perceive that this is a modest understatement of the truth.

In the second place, Job meets this argument by showing his friends that he is in as full agreement with them about the frailty and ignorance of man as he is about the wisdom and power of God. And here again he betters their instruction. But not only does Job completely outclass his friends in his descriptions of the weakness and limitations of humanity, but there is probably nothing in the whole range of literature which equals, alike in their pathetic truthfulness and in their poetic beauty, the moving pictures which he paints of the state of man in these respects. This strong statement is fully proved by many passages in the speeches of Job, but especially by that long and wonderful passage in his reply to the first speech of Zophar, which begins with the words—" Man that is born of a woman is of few days and full of trouble. He cometh forth like a flower, and is cut down : he fleeth also as a shadow, and continueth not."

But in the third place, although Job so fully indorses both of these premises of the friends, he utterly rejects the deduction which they draw from them, namely, that it is necessarily presump tuous impiety for a man to make any criticism on the providence of God. He does so upon two grounds. The first of these is the legitimate claims of creatureship upon the Creator, which he is confident that God Himself will respect, however his friends may despise them. He does not believe in the cold and relentless concentration of Omnipotence which his friends offer him for a God. He believes that God has a respect and a desire towards the work of His own hands.

His second ground for rejecting this conclusion of his friends is that in no other way can he be true to his own moral consciousness. If the orthodox theory of his friends is right, and the only one that is to be entertained, then what Job has to say is that it is simply not possible to harmonise it with many of the facts of human life in general, and with many of the facts of his own experience in particular. Now they were all agreed that God was directly responsible for these facts of Providence. Therefore Job argued conclusively that it was their theory and not his criticism which did dishonour to God. For himself, he declared that he could not conveniently shut his eyes to these facts as his friends were prepared to do. Therefore he felt compelled to criticise, unless he was prepared to be false to the clear dictates

JOB'S REPLY TO HIS FRIENDS 153

of his own conscience; and so he could not be silent, but must speak in the bitterness of his soul.

This leads Job on to the third stage of his defence, in which he discusses the great problem of justification. Here he reaches the very heart of the argument and the crux of the whole debate. He does not deal with the problem in any narrow or one-sided way, but on the contrary, with a remarkable breadth and comprehensiveness. The foundation of all that his friends had to say here was that God was just and that He would by no means fail to reward both the wicked and the righteous according to their deserts. Now this great truth was also the foundation of Job's religion, and to it he gives whole-hearted assent. That had always been the dearest belief of Job's heart, and it was indeed the one hope that remained to him now, when he was being so falsely judged by men, even by his own best friends.

" Shall not the Judge of all the earth do right ? " That had ever been the very key-stone of the whole arch of his faith. His friends could not hold that fundamental truth with more passionate earnestness than he did. But they made most cruel applications of that great truth to Job's recent and present experiences. They suggested that if his children had perished it could only be because they were wicked, and that if he himself was now suffering extraordinary misery it could only be because he had been guilty of extraordinary sin. But Job knew, as his friends could not, that he had no such sins to confess as would explain why he was being subjected to such suffering, while his friends were exempt from it. Here, then, Job was face to face with a deep dilemma. With all his heart he desired to continue his faith in the absolute justice of God. But it appeared as if it would be impossible for him to do this unless he not only denied that the facts of Providence were what he knew they were, but also unless he deliberately lied against the conscious integrity of his own life.

It was this terrible problem of personal justification that pressed so hard upon the spirit of Job. It was a problem which he could in no way solve, turn it which way he would. He knew that the argument of his friends was wrong, but how to set it right he could not find. " How can man be just with God ? " He makes a great and passionate endeavour to answer that deep question, but all the while it is only too plain how bitterly conscious he is that he is attempting

JOB'S REPLY TO HIS FRIENDS 155

the impossible. Nay, Job perceives that his effort to find how man can appear just before God leads him inevitably to the consideration of a still deeper question—How can the ways of God be justified to man?

In the discussion of these two great cognate questions his mind vibrates between a tendency to despair and a steadfast determination to maintain his faith in the justice and goodness of God in the face of all appearances to the contrary. In dealing with this central subject it is notable that Job often finds the arguments of his friends so shallow or so false that he ceases to answer them directly, and then he glides away into a kind of soliloquy in which he follows the deeper windings of his own thoughts on this profound theme. These deeper aspects of the problem which arose from the strange moral contradiction between the doctrine of God's absolute justice and the awful but undeniable facts of life seemed to have no existence for his friends, but they had an overwhelming fascination for the mind of Job.

We know from many statements which Job makes that he did not regard either himself or his children as sinless. But on the other hand, against the cruel and unjust assumption of his friends that it was the extraordinary wickedness of his children that justified their utter destruction, his whole soul rose in revolt. For he knew the character and life of his children as they could not, and he knew that their assumption was untrue. As for himself, he knew that through his whole life he had tried so to live that he would be just before God.

Yet according to the orthodox theology, which he also had hitherto believed, the terrible sufferings with which God now overwhelmed him were terrible most of all for this, that they were the divine verdict proving that all his moral endeavour had been an utter failure. Instead of treating him as a good man, God was treating him as an extraordinarily wicked one. The question that rose before the mind of Job, therefore, was this—How could he or any man be made just before a God who treated such a man as Job knew himself to be in such a way ? If he had failed so utterly, was there any way by which any man might reasonably hope to succeed ?

Now there are three things which lead Job in considering this question to answer it in the

JOB'S REPLY TO HIS FRIENDS 157

negative. These things, observe, are all in God, although they are considered in relation to things in man.

The first of these things is God's perfect knowledge. This is considered in relation to human sin. If God is pleased to contend with a man, says Job, he cannot answer Him one of a thousand. He remembers that God is " wise in heart "; and here we are to remember that to the ancient the heart was the seat of the intellect as well as of the affections. Job is not free from the consciousness of guilt, though his friends generally treat him as if he were. His own heart condemns him; and he knows that God is greater than his heart and knows all things. No man can look back upon his life without seeing a thousand things which he is ashamed to see, and which he would abolish the very memory of, if only that were possible. Job felt this, and he felt that if God was to deal strictly concerning these things in any man's life no man could give Him an answer for one in a thousand. Moreover, he felt that God's knowledge of every man's life was infinitely more perfect than the man's own. Therefore there could be no justification possible on that side for any man.

The second thing that oppressed Job in this

connection was the awful inaccessibility of God in relation to man. He dwells upon this thought as if it had a tremendous fascination for him, until it brings a deep gloom over his spirit. How could man ever hope to get near enough to so great and so mysterious a Being as to deal with Him about his justification; or if God chose to crush him in his feebleness how could frail man resist the exercise of God's tremendous power against him? The manifestations of God's power and majesty in the earthquake, and in the storm, and in the motions of the heavenly bodies, profoundly impressed the mind of Job and made him feel his own utter insignificance in presence of such a Being, and how remote was the hope of any direct intercourse with Him concerning those perplexing thoughts that so distressed him. "Which removeth the mountains and they know it not, when He overturneth them in His anger: Which shaketh the earth out of her place, and the pillars thereof tremble: Which commandeth the sun and it riseth not, and sealeth up the stars: Which alone stretcheth out the heavens, and treadeth upon the waves of the sea." Yet again and again Job gives expression to his intense desire for that direct

JOB'S REPLY TO HIS FRIENDS 159

intercourse with God which he finds it so impossible to obtain, and declares his assurance that if only he could obtain it God would treat him in a very different way from the way in which he was being treated by his friends.

But the third great obstacle which stands in the way of man's justification before God Job finds to be the most serious of all. It is that the facts of life often seem to indicate that in His dealings with men God is sometimes at least governed by an unreasoning and indiscriminating caprice. It is here that the great question emerges which Job perceives to be the other side of this part of the argument, namely—How can the ways of God with man be justified to the moral sense of man? And this is where the accepted orthodoxy of the three friends most conspicuously breaks down.

Unlike his superficial friends Job has made up his mind to face the facts, however they may baffle him. He looks abroad upon human society and he sees three things at which he will not wink, but which he will state clearly in their bald truth. First, the wicked are not rewarded according to their wickedness. On the contrary, he sees only too plainly what his friends conveniently ignore, but what the psalmists afterwards also saw in Jerusalem, and what we can still see in any modern city, that the wicked often spread themselves and prosper like green bay trees. Not only is vengeance not executed speedily against an evil work, but often it is not executed at all, so that often the wicked have no bands even in their death.

The second thing that Job saw was that in the devastating earthquake and in the overwhelming storm the great forces of nature, which, like every Semite, he thought of not as impersonal but as under God's immediate control, indiscriminately destroyed the innocent with the wicked. To Job's strained imagination it even appeared as if in these great calamities God sometimes seemed like a wild beast stealthily watching to pounce upon His helpless victim. " Behold," he exclaims, " He seizeth the prey, who can hinder Him ? Who will say unto Him, what doest Thou ? God will not withdraw His anger."

This is a bitter thought to Job, and one which depresses and perplexes him exceedingly, as it has done many others since. " It is all one," he cries despondingly, " therefore I say He

JOB'S REPLY TO HIS FRIENDS 161

destroyeth the perfect and the wicked: If the scourge slay suddenly He will mock at the trial of the innocent. The earth is given into the hand of the wicked: He covereth the faces of the judges thereof; if it be not He, who then is it?" Here Job suggests that it seems as if God must be responsible for all the evil that is in the world, even for the wrong judgment of the unjust judge. If the theology of his friends was still to be accepted he could see no other solution that would square with the unquestionable facts; and he was right.

But the third difficulty which Job saw in the way in seeking to justify the moral government of God he perceived to be the most terrible anomaly of all. It was that the righteous man, far from being specially blessed was often made the subject of extraordinary suffering. It is in this connection that Job deals with the theory of the divine correction put forward by his friends. He has no quarrel with that theory so far as it is consistent with facts; but his objection is that it by no means covers all the sufferings of men in the providence of God, and that in particular when it is applied to his own case it is nothing better than a bitter mockery. He feels that his friends confuse gracious correction with serverest judgment. He knows that it is quite consistent with God's justice and goodness that He should correct a good man when he errs; but what he wants his friends to explain is how God overwhelms a good man with calamity and suffering, while He lavishes health and prosperity upon an openly wicked one. They cannot answer that, and Job feels in the earnest contemplation of his own case as if it shut him up to the conclusion that God is cruelly unjust. "He breaketh me with a tempest," he exclaims, "and multiplieth my wounds without cause. He will not suffer me to take my breath but filleth me with bitterness."

Job is resolved to be frankly truthful, not only about the facts of God's general providence, but also about the facts of his own experience in relation to that providence. He knows that he is not the wicked man which, according to the theory of his friends, the great suffering that God is imposing upon him makes him appear to be, and his whole soul rises in revolt against this unjust misrepresentation of his life. Therefore, he says, with a defiant indignation—"I am perfect; I regard not myself; I despise my life."

JOB'S REPLY TO HIS FRIENDS 163

He is determined to speak the truth in scorn of consequence. Though God slay him for the attitude which he assumes he will not subscribe to the false arguments of his friends, even although God seems to indorse them : he will not take refuge in what he knows to be a lie.

It is when his case presents itself to his mind in this aspect, when he sees in front of him his hopeless misery, and on his left hand the shallowness and falseness of the reasonings of his friends, and on his right hand the cruel injustice of his God—it is then that the argument of Job sinks to its lowest depths and he utters things that cannot be justified, although even then we still find much to admire in his words. These dark moods have well-marked features.

One of these features is fierce denunciation of his friends for their false advocacy for God. " Ye are forgers of lies," he cries ; " ye are all physicians of no value. O that ye would altogether hold your peace ! And it should be your wisdom." " Will ye speak unrighteously for God, and talk deceitfully for him ? " he exclaims again. " Will ye respect His person ? Will ye contend for God ? " Job saw that his friends did not hesitate to ignore or deny the facts which were against that orthodox creed, so comfortable for them, so cruel for him, and that they were even ready to twist the truth here and there if that seemed the only way to save their creed and the character of God too. It was this immorality in the service of religion that moved Job to righteous indignation. He scorned the wise and prudent saws by which they propped up their rotten arguments, even as Christ afterwards scorned the commentaries of the Rabbis that made void the law of God. "Your memorable sayings," cried Job, "are proverbs of ashes, your defences are defences of clay."

And how often has this same unworthy course been followed in religious matters since the days of Job? Whenever some new light requires some modification of the old creed, whether the light come from the progress of science, or whether it come from a more thorough knowledge of the Holy Scriptures, then men have ever shown themselves prone to fall into the temptation to "speak unrighteously for God and to talk deceitfully for Him." But this ostrich policy is not only most foolish and most dangerous, it is also most irreligious. It is, as Job says, an attempt to respect God's person.

JOB'S REPLY TO HIS FRIENDS 165

These friends of his talked as if God's title to worship were founded on wisdom and power alone. But Job shows that the moral consciousness of man requires that his God be not only wise and mighty, but above all righteous and just, using His wisdom and power for equitable ends. He confesses that he cannot harmonise such a conception of God with the facts of life as he knows them; but he is so sure that this conception of God is the only right one that he threatens his friends with the judgment of God Himself because they have dared to argue unrighteously on His behalf. "He will surely reprove you," he says, "if ye do secretly show favour. Shall not His excellency make you afraid, and His dread fall upon you?" This is a warning which is needed by many men of every generation.

Another feature of these dark moods is the desperate boldness with which Job seeks to justify his own honest but seemingly irreverent search after the truth. "Wherefore should I take my flesh in my teeth?" he asks, "and put my life in mine hand? Though He slay me, yet will I wait for Him: nevertheless, I will maintain my ways before Him. This also shall be my salvation." There is a splendid courage in this championship for the truth which cannot fail to command the admiration of all true souls. There is no insolent impiety in this heroic boldness, but there is a determined earnestness for the victory of truth, and there is also a genuine faith in the goodness and justice of God.

Job vividly realises that his case is desperate, and he knows that appearances are all against him. But he knows also that when his friends assumed secret sins in his life that would account for his terrible sufferings they were building on lies ; and he believes with all his heart that their assertions as to what God was doing and would do concerning him were as destitute of any true foundation. He believes that his true salvation consists, not in subscribing to the false theories of his friends who enlisted their invention in playing the advocate for God, but in holding fast to the facts, with all their perplexing mystery, and in waiting for God's own explanation of these.

He did not, indeed, doubt that it was really God who was imposing all this affliction upon him, nor could he find any just reason why He should

JOB'S REPLY TO HIS FRIENDS 167

do so. It seemed to him from the steady progress that his awful disease was making that God meant it to end in death, and we must not forget that the Sheol beyond death was to his mind a region of uncertain shadows. Nevertheless, whatever happened, he would not abandon the truth as he knew it. Though God should slay him, yet he would wait for God. He did not believe that there was any other true hope, and he did believe that from that direction alone would his salvation come. If anybody could prove that God was really the kind of Being that his friends were representing Him to be, and not the kind of Being that he believed Him to be, then Job was ready to hold his peace and to give up the ghost.

The attitude of Job here, therefore, although it is most rational in the truest meaning of that word, is also in reality a splendid exhibition of faith in the goodness of the character of God and in the righteousness of His methods of work, even when these methods were shrouded in darkest mystery. And this, we should observe, is the distinction of Job's attitude here. It is always quite easy to state the problems of Providence with a rash impiety, and with either infidel or atheistic deductions; but what is not easy is to feel these problems bearing with a terrible pressure upon your own experience, and yet to say, "Though He slay me, yet will I trust in Him." But to that great height did the faith of Job sometimes arise, even when the darkness was deepest around him.

A third feature of these dark moods of Job is the despair to which they at times reduce him. This temporary despair finds expression in his speeches in two strikingly different forms. First, in a rebellious indignation against God, in which his language often hovers on the verge of blasphemy and his mind seems almost in a state of utter apostacy. It is at such times that he really "darkens counsel by words without knowledge." And looking back upon these words after he has been reproved by the divine voice out of the whirlwind he has to confess—"I have uttered that which I understood not, things too wonderful for me, which I knew not."

And yet, even in such wild passages, spoken when his whole nature is in a state of tumult and quivering under a sense of mystery and pain and wrong, the very form in which he generally

JOB'S REPLY TO HIS FRIENDS 169

expresses his charges against God shows that he does not himself believe them, but that they are the somewhat wild expression of his own utter perplexity and of his passionate desire to reach the truth which he feels so much beyond him. And even we, with all the great new light that has come to us in Christ, still find the darkness deep enough when we are brought face to face with these same old questions in some new form. Why, then, should we wonder that they so overwhelmed the mind of Job in his much darker days? And neither need we wonder that although God blamed him for being over-bold and too self-confident, He freely forgave him and richly blessed him at the last.

The other form in which this transient despair of Job expresses itself is hopeless lamentation. Again and again in the course of the discussion, after he has demolished the arguments of his friends, but has nevertheless been utterly baffled in his earnest search for some adequate solution to the problem of his own terrible condition, he breaks away into those melancholy threnodies in which he dwells with an overwhelming pathos and power upon the different aspects of

170 AFFLICTIONS OF THE RIGHTEOUS

his misery of body and sorrow of mind. These threnodies are full of profound sadness, of keen distress, and of pathetic self-pity. They do all that it is possible for words to do as the instruments of great genius in painting the picture of a man who has reached the utmost extremity of misery and desolation, and for whom no ray of light or gleam of hope remains.

This brings us to the final stage in Job's presentation of his case. That is his declaration of his faith in God and in his own future, notwithstanding all that would seem to make such faith impossible. I have said that Job's dark moods were temporary, and that his darkest utterances in them did not truly represent his mind. But this is not the whole truth; for there is a deep connection between the darkest parts of his experience and the brightest outbursts of his faith.

There is true philosophy, and there is also moral necessity in this, in relation to such a man as Job. For the true soul out of the deepest realisation of need springs the victorious faith that conquers the difficulties and transforms the darkness of life. It was in one of his darkest moods

JOB'S REPLY TO HIS FRIENDS 171

that the wonderful thought of a "daysman" came to Job. Referring to God's inaccessibility he said—"He is not a man, as I am, that I should answer Him, that we should come together in judgment. There is no daysman betwixt us, that might lay his hand upon us both."

Of course it would be quite illegitimate to read into this saying of Job any definite suggestion of the incarnation; yet it is a very remarkable utterance as expressing his deep longing for a "goël," an umpire, or mediator between himself and God; and it is particularly impressive as springing right out of the heart of Job's deep need, and as being the only means he can conceive of that would set him right with God and justify him before his fellow-men. He felt that he needed one who would come nearer to him than any of his friends, with an understanding sympathy, and with all the tenderness of a true human brotherhood; and yet one who could lay his hand upon God as well as upon himself, and who would have power to reconcile because he would have divine authority and grace as well as human sympathy and fellowship. Job could see no other way of salvation.

172 AFFLICTIONS OF THE RIGHTEOUS

We see the same thing illustrated in a still more remarkable manner in Job's second answer to Bildad. Here the sufferer is in one of his darkest moods. The speech is almost wholly occupied with a most distressing description of his awful condition, which ends in the heart-moving appeal— "Have pity upon me, have pity upon me, O ye my friends; for the hand of God hath touched me. Why do ye persecute me as God, and are not satisfied with my flesh?" But it is just here, when everything is blackest, that his faith, springing up like the rainbow in the cloud, and using the very elements of his calamity, as the rainbow uses the elements of the storm, as the instruments of its glory, shines with a marvellous splendour.

He introduces his most striking declaration of the faith thus born within him with words of singular solemnity, which strongly express his desire for a permanent record of this declaration, as being incomparably the most important thing which he has to say—" O that my words were now written! O that they were inscribed in a book! That with an iron pen and lead they were graven in the rock for ever! For I know that my Redeemer (goël) liveth, and that He

JOB'S REPLY TO HIS FRIENDS 173

shall stand up at last upon the earth; and after my skin has been thus destroyed, yet from my flesh shall I see God: whom I shall see for myself, and mine eyes shall behold, and not another."

This magnificent burst of faith is the very climax and crown of Job's argument, and it is also the real crisis of the whole book. What does it mean? To find in it merely the expression of a hope that he will be cured of his physical malady is to give a miserably inadequate interpretation of it. To import into it the whole Christian doctrine of the resurrection is to err as much on the other side. The truth lies between. Job has no clear view of how God will achieve his salvation; but this great utterance is an emphatic declaration of his conviction that God will certainly find some way to vindicate and to reward His suffering servant at last, and that the chief element in that reward will be a deeper, happier intercourse with God.

His faith is firmly founded upon past experience of communion with God. He knows that his Redeemer lives, He himself expects death. But his Redeemer will live on *as* his Redeemer.

He perceives that this immediately involves his own redemption. Neither he nor God can otherwise be justified. The great moral necessity gives energy and certitude to his faith. Notwithstanding death, through death, and beyond death, the vindication and the reward *must* come. Thus we see nothing less in this sublime utterance of Job than the seed of what was so gloriously brought to the full flower in the teaching of Him who brought life and immortality to light, and which He crystallised in such sayings as these—" God is not the God of the dead but of the living." " Because I live, ye shall live also."

It is not necessary for our present purpose to follow the later speeches of Job in detail, especially as they largely consist of emphatic restatements of arguments which he has already used, in particular the great argument from the facts of life. It is notable, however, that while his friends in their later speeches attack Job with increasing fierceness, he, on the other hand, after his great declaration of faith, grows more mild and humble in his spirit, follows their arguments less closely because he feels their unfairness and futility, but seeks to draw closer to God.

JOB'S REPLY TO HIS FRIENDS 175

He is distressed above all because he can find no access to God, but in these later speeches he comforts himself with the thought that although he cannot find God, God is ever watching over him, and that the end is sure. " Behold I go forward; but He is not there; and backward, but I cannot perceive Him; on the left hand where He doth work, but I cannot behold Him: He hideth Himself on the right hand, that I cannot see Him. But *He knoweth* the way that *I* take; when He hath tried me, I shall come forth as gold."

There is special difficulty in interpreting the last speech of Job which begins with the twenty-sixth and ends with the thirty-first chapter. Here is raised for the first time the question of the integrity of the book, a question which is raised again, and more seriously, in connection with the speech of Elihu. It is suggested that there is dislocation and confusion in these chapters, that part of them should be put into the mouth of one of Job's friends, that in the twenty-seventh chapter Job is parodying the statements of his friends, that chapter twenty-eight is to be taken as a choral interlude after the manner of the chorus in the Greek dramas, and that both of these chapters are insertions by a later hand.

But these suggestions are more or less fanciful and are not supported by a close study of the text. The only one has that much weight is that which points out the apparent opposition between some of the ideas in this speech and ideas expressed in the other speeches of Job. But this opposition is not absolute. Job never said that the wicked were never punished, but only that they were not always punished according to their wickedness. It is clear from the phrase, "And Job again took up his parable and said," at the beginning of the twenty-seventh chapter, and by the repetition of that phrase at the beginning of the twenty-ninth chapter, that the poet meant to represent the friends as utterly failing in the debate, and to show that Job is left the undisputed master of the field. This explains the length of Job's final speech, which may rather be regarded as three successive speeches.

The argument of Job, then, against his three friends, taken as a whole, may be summed up thus—

I. With regard to their theory of the Providence

JOB'S REPLY TO HIS FRIENDS 177

of God in general, Job proves to a demonstration that the assumptions upon which it is based are contrary to undeniable facts; for—

1. The righteous are often not prosperous, but the reverse.
2. The unrighteous are often not unprosperous, but the reverse.

II. With regard to the application of their theory of Providence to his own case, the argument of Job does not reach a demonstration, but approaches it; thus—

1. He points to his life-long outward conduct as proof of his integrity.
2. He points to his long-continued prosperity to prove that, according to the theory of his friends, God had, for many years, treated him as righteous.
3. He vehemently denies the specific charges of wrong-doing which they make against him, and defies them to prove one of them.
4. He rejects with indignation their insinuations of secret sins such as would account for his distress in accordance with their theory.
5. Notwithstanding his bursts of rebellion against God, induced by his misery, he

M

persistently appeals for the judgment of God against the false judgment of men, and declares himself willing to suffer all that he may deserve to suffer, God Himself being judge.

III. With regard to the application of the theory of his friends to the justification of the ways of God with men—

1. Job shows that he is not less but more profoundly concerned about the justification of God's ways with men than they are.
2. He shows that his method of dealing with the providence of God is really more honouring to God than theirs, for they sought to whitewash God's providence, to forge lies and speak deceitfully for Him; whereas he at least acknowledged the facts, and sought to deal honestly with them.
3. Building upon his own conscious integrity he perceives and argues that the justification of God is involved in his own justification. This is one of the deepest perceptions in the book.
4. Finally, therefore, although he cannot penetrate the darkness by which he is

JOB'S REPLY TO HIS FRIENDS 179

surrounded on every side, yet he believes that the Eternal Light shines on behind the darkness, and he is resolved to wait, although in sadness and in pain,

"'Till on the glimmering limit, far withdrawn,
God makes Himself an awful rose of dawn.

CHAPTER VIII

JOB'S EXPOSTULATIONS WITH GOD

IN the course of this great discussion between Job and his friends, he again and again becomes so keenly conscious of the unfairness and the utter futility of their arguments against him that he, feeling deeply how "vain is the help of man," turns away from them and their "proverbs of ashes," and makes his appeal directly to God Himself. These appeals, however, are carried on in the presence of Job's friends, and they are evidently intended by the Hebrew poet to exhibit the better way of dealing with the moral problem of a good man's suffering, as opposed to the false way of the friends, against which Job is always protesting.

There is no refuge of lies, and no speaking unrighteously and deceitfully for God in these remarkable passages. Job orders his cause before God with an amazing boldness, which sometimes lacks due reverence, and with frank declarations

JOB'S EXPOSTULATIONS WITH GOD 181

of inexplicable facts, mingling his strangely complex appeals with petitions, remonstrances, laments, and here and there with daring flights of faith, which are the prophecies of his ultimate deliverance. These passages are among the greatest in this great book. They throb with a profound pathos. They are wonderfully rich in that high poetic beauty which has all the indescribable fascination of great genius. They glow with an intense feeling which is associated with a most vivid spiritual penetration. There is a singular felicity and propriety in their imagery, and the exquisite fitness of the language in which each successive idea is set forth fixes them in the memory as enduring pictures there.

Job grounds his appeal to God upon the basis of undeniable fact, fact that is within the circle of his own personal experience. That fact he relates to the accepted theory of Providence, and then he feels that he is justified in reproaching God for what appears to be His pitiless persecution of himself without any adequate cause. "I will speak in the anguish of my spirit," he says, "I will complain in the bitterness of my soul. Am I a sea, or a sea-monster, that Thou settest a watch over me? When I say, My bed shall comfort me, my couch shall ease my complaint; then Thou scarest me with dreams, and terrifiest me through visions; so that my soul chooseth strangling, and death rather than these my bones. I loathe my life; I would not live alway: let me alone; for my days are vanity."

In these words Job reveals a passionate sense of injustice in relation to his sufferings. He feels as if he were being treated as a very different person from what he is, as if he were almost dangerous to the peace of the world. There is also a pathetic self-pity in his complaint. There is no cessation of his misery and pain. When he is awake the actual realities of his condition make life an insupportable burden to him; but God persecutes him even in the realms of sleep with such frightful visions as to make him long for death with a new earnestness. He broods upon this strange divine persecution until he sometimes thinks that God is treating him more as if he were a wild beast than a man. "If my head exalt itself," he says, "Thou huntest me as a lion: and again Thou shewest Thyself marvellous upon me. Thou renewest Thy wit-

JOB'S EXPOSTULATIONS WITH GOD 183

nesses against me, and increasest Thine indignation upon me."

He thinks of himself mournfully as being worn down to the very dust of death by this unceasing persecution of God. It is a thing which no man could resist, and from which no human being could escape, and so it fills him with an utter hopelessness. He tells God that the treatment which He is meting out to him is filling him with blank despair. " The waters wear the stones," he says, " The overflowings thereof wash away the dust of the earth ; and Thou destroyest the hope of man. Thou prevailest for ever against him, and he passeth ; Thou changest his countenance, and sendest him away."

As we have seen, the explanation which his friends gave him of all this severe treatment he was suffering at the hands of God was that he was an exceptionally wicked man. Job resented with intense feeling what he knew to be the grievous injustice of this explanation. And because he could give no other, and because God seemed to take sides with the unjust against him, he could not help feeling that God was treating him with a settled cruelty ; and he frankly stated his conviction to God. " Thou art turned to be cruel to me," he said, "with the might of Thy hand Thou persecutest me. Thou liftest me up to the wind, Thou causest me to ride upon it; and Thou dissolvest me in the storm. For I know that Thou wilt bring me to death, and to the house appointed for all living."

But in his expostulations with God Job passes from the consideration of how God's treatment of him affects himself to the more important thought of how that treatment affects the character and reputation of God himself. He begs God to withdraw His hand from him, to give him a little ease from his terrible pain, and not to overwhelm him by the greatness of His majesty and power, that he may be able to concentrate his powers upon the discussion of his case. "What is man," he asks, "that Thou shouldst magnify him, and that Thou shouldst visit him every morning, and try him every moment? How long wilt Thou not look away from me, nor let me alone till I swallow down my spittle?"

Job is deeply impressed by the thought that it is quite unworthy of a Being so great as God to use His resistless power continually for the mere purpose of torturing and finally crushing so weak

JOB'S EXPOSTULATIONS WITH GOD 185

and helpless a creature as himself. This is a line of conduct, he sees, that has a great bearing upon God as well as upon himself. Will not God, therefore, be moved by that consideration, at least, to alter His treatment of His suffering servant? "Is it good unto Thee," he asks, " that Thou shouldest oppress, that Thou shouldest despise the work of Thine hands? and shine upon the counsel of the wicked?"

Job is surprised that God should select so insignificant a thing as himself for His enemy. He wonders why He should pursue such a worm with such relentless punishment; for what kind of glory can God hope to get out of his destruction? Job demands an answer to that question also from God Himself. "Wilt thou harass a driven leaf?" he asks, "And wilt Thou pursue the dry stubble?—Thou puttest my feet also in the stocks, and markest all my paths; Thou drawest Thee a line about the soles of my feet: though I am like a rotten thing that consumeth, like a garment that is moth-eaten." This language evidently refers to the ravages of his dreadful disease in his body, and we cannot be just to Job unless we ever keep these in mind, and remember not only the bearing which they have on the central theme of the book, but also the effects which they could not fail to produce on the mind of Job itself.

He gives wonderfully varied expression to his sense of utter wretchedness and helpless weakness. Over against this he shows a profound sense of the awful power and majesty of God. The thought of that power, however, gives him no comfort, but rather oppresses him with a sense of bewildering fear; because he is convinced that it is God who is the supreme cause of his present frightful experience, and that He is using His awful power, not to help him, but to torture him, and to make him a thing beneath contempt. Job wonders what all other beings who have power to judge will think of such a use of omnipotence against impotence. Can there be anything in it to add to the glory of God ? Must there not rather be much in it to detract from that glory ?

But Job pursues this bold line of thought a stage further when he ventures to remind God that, after all, the Creator has some responsibilities in relation to His creatures, and that His creatures have some legitimate claims upon Him whose conduct must be the supreme standard of morality by virtue of His having called them into being. In view of his present condition Job does not see why he should

JOB'S EXPOSTULATIONS WITH GOD 187

ever have been born at all. If this was all that God had in view in his creation, then, viewed as a work of God, that creation has been a complete failure, which, both in regard to wisdom and power, reflects serious discredit upon God.

After a deep and honest search into his own life Job can find nothing there to account for his fearful state. He therefore throws back the responsibility for that state upon God himself as his Creator. He feels that he is mere clay in the hands of the potter. What can he do to alter the destiny which God has appointed for him? The power is God's, and therefore the responsibility is also God's. Thus Job argues that the only way in which God can be justified for bringing him into being at all is by exerting His power anew to deliver him from his present condition. So long as God refuses to do this, but goes on using His power to oppress him as He is doing, Job maintains that his very existence is a standing reproach to God. Therefore he further expostulates with God—" Thine hands have framed me and fashioned me together round about; yet Thou dost destroy me. Remember, I beseech Thee, that Thou hast fashioned me as clay; and wilt thou bring me into dust again?" Perhaps we have here the seed of that fine flower of thought which is set forth with Christian assurance by Tennyson—

> " Thou wilt not leave us in the dust,
> Thou madest man : he knows not why :
> He thinks he was not made to die ;
> And Thou hast made him ; Thou art just."

But Tennyson, like ourselves, lived in the days of the Gospel of the resurrection ; and we must not forget how much darker were the days of Job. We have already seen that on rare occasions the expression of Job's faith reached even a higher level than this of Tennyson ; but we cannot wonder that he frequently sank to far lower levels of doubt and fear and dark suspicion of God. " Hast Thou not poured me out as milk, and curdled me like cheese ? " he asks. " Thou hast clothed me with skin and flesh, and knit me together with bones and sinews. Thou hast granted me life and favour, and Thy visitation hath preserved my spirit. Yet these things Thou didst hide in Thine heart ; I know that this is with Thee." Job felt as if the past favour of God were merely fleeting and transitory, and that all the while He had been hiding in His heart these cruel purposes against him, and that now in all the agonies he was enduring God was accomplishing His ultimate designs upon him.

JOB'S EXPOSTULATIONS WITH GOD 189

Now this great problem, in which we have helpless human suffering contrasted with seemingly overbearing omnipotence, is one to which some of the greatest thinkers have addressed themselves with all their strength. The great Hebrew singers of the Psalter and the chief prophets of Israel again and again recur to it. It had also an irresistible fascination for the master minds of Greece. The great Greek poet, Æschylus, dealt with it in his "Prometheus Bound," in which he presents us with an impressive picture of a heroic martyrdom under an omnipotent tyranny. That tragic picture is strongly coloured with the early mythology of Greece, but the central problem is unmistakable.

Sophocles, another of the greatest among the Greek poets, treats exhaustively of the same theme from a different standpoint in the experiences of his hero, Œdipus, and he handles the subject with great philosophic power as well as rare poetic beauty. But, after all, the solution he arrives at is no solution, because it is so utterly inadequate to human need; for it is mere helpless, hopeless patience on the one side and inflexible fate on the other. Our own great poet, Shelley, in his "Prometheus Unbound," returned to the problem as presented by Æschylus; but with all his genius he made so poor a use of the new light in Christ that he came no nearer to the true solution than the ancient Greek. His Prometheus is merely a proud, rebellious soul, who first misconceives, and then revolts against the all-ruling Providence of the world, and whose one hope is that he may somehow conquer God at last.

Byron also, in his terrible tragedy of "Cain," attempted the same theme on the basis of the early Bible narrative, and handled it as if he held a brief for Satan. Some of the speeches of Lucifer in this work reach a most daring height of impiety, and yet in the sequel they turn out to be a mere baying at the moon. In more recent times also, Matthew Arnold, in what is distinctly his greatest poem, "Empedocles on Etna," exerted his genius to its utmost capacity on this same enduring problem. There are many gems of thought, and much rich philosophy in that remarkable work; but again the conclusion is found to be weak and insufficient even to the point of absurdity. Empedocles is a misanthrope; he says many wise and true things about human life, yet we feel that while he is all alive to life's sadness he is deaf and blind to life's gladness and life's hope. And when

JOB'S EXPOSTULATIONS WITH GOD 191

he ends all his musings by jumping into the crater the hero is discovered to be, after all, merely a feeble coward, who had no proper understanding either of the blessings of life or the meaning of human death. For even if argument were wholly wanting we would yet profoundly feel that to prescribe suicide for the help of life's sorrows is verily to give us a stone when we ask for bread.

Now when we compare these striking works with these great speeches of Job, wherein he so boldly expostulates with God, we find many points of contact, but Job's speeches are superbly distinguished from them all by the attitude of the sufferer towards God. The Prometheus of Æschylus and Shelley regards God as his enemy, and his only hope is in the dethronement of the deity. The Œdipus of Sophocles has really no God to appeal to, for his deity is himself the subject of inflexible fate, and all that remains to the sufferer is therefore a helpless, hopeless stoicism. The Cain of Byron is a being whose opposition to the Almighty is yet more pronounced than that of Prometheus, and his sullen subjection is merely a policy of despair. The Empedocles of Arnold, on the other hand, practically appoints himself his own God,

192 AFFLICTIONS OF THE RIGHTEOUS

and completely abandons the hope of all supernatural help as he sings—

> "Once read thine own breast right,
>   And thou hast done with fears ;
> Man gets no other light,
>   Search he a thousand years.
> Sink in thyself, and ask,
>   What ails thee at that shrine."

But Job is distinguished from all these in that, while he sometimes feels as if God were treating him as His enemy, yet his faith and his hope, amid all his deep perplexity, are ever in God himself alone. His questions, indeed, are often amazingly fierce and bold. None were ever more daring, although they might easily be more impious. God seems terribly overbearing in His awful providence, and so Job cries again and again with vehement impatience that if God will not deliver him He ought at least to let him alone. But amid all this bold interrogation of his Maker it is always very plain that Job still feels God to be his one necessary Friend, even while He seems an enemy ; and even when life's mystery is at the darkest, and his pain is greatest, Job still says— " Though He slay me, yet will I trust in Him." This is indeed a very great distinction ; for just

JOB'S EXPOSTULATIONS WITH GOD 193

to trust in God amid all darkness and all mystery is, after all, the one thing that meets the greatest and the deepest human need.

But Job reaches a further stage in his expostulations with God when he prays to God to grant unto him immediately the boon of death. If to satisfy some unknown end of God he had to be born; and if, for some further inscrutable reason, God would not deliver him from his present miseries; if he cannot even obtain a little respite from his sorrows that he may have some returning glimpse of rest and peace in fulfilling the residue of his hireling day of life; then why should not the gift of immediate death be granted to one in his condition?

According to the faith of Job's day nothing could be more melancholy than the state of the dead in Sheol. Existence in that most gloomy region was conceived of as more a dream than a life. There a man was a mere shadow of his former self. He was supposed to be cut off from all intercourse with life, whether human or divine. Sheol was a dark limbo of isolation and forgetfulness from which there was no hope of escape. But it is most interesting to note how in this respect also Job rises above the faith of his time. His friends were

N

dreadfully shocked at his prayers for death, and sought to show him that a return to temporal prosperity was rather the thing for which he ought to pray. Job, however, returns to his prayers for death again and again. " O that Thou wouldest hide me in Sheol," he cries to God, " that Thou wouldest keep me secret until Thy wrath be past, that Thou wouldest appoint me a set time, and remember me ! If a man die shall he live again ? All the days of my warfare would I wait, till my release should come. Thou shouldest call, and I would answer Thee : Thou wouldest have a desire to the work of thine hands."

It is notable that Job does not here, like some of the later psalmists, pray that at death he should make a transit over Sheol into the immediate presence of God, there to enjoy in a fuller degree the communion and favour of God. Job believed that God was angry with him, and he saw in his present misery the proof of that anger, but his idea of God prevented him from believing that such anger could last for ever. His vision of reconciliation and a subsequent blessed immortality was begotten of the consciousness of his own utter need and his faith in God's good mercy.

JOB'S EXPOSTULATIONS WITH GOD 195

Job supported his prayers for death upon three grounds. First, because it would be a great relief to himself; for he felt the burden of his miseries to be insupportable. This plea reveals his secret faith that, notwithstanding all his terrible troubles, God has a real desire for his well-being. Secondly, because his case with regard to this life seemed to be utterly hopeless. He believed himself to be dying, but his death was appallingly slow. Thirdly, because he felt that he had nothing to fear, but on the contrary much to hope for from death; for he knew that he had not denied the words of the Holy One; and he believed that beyond death God would call for him, and he would answer God.

This reveals the fact that however mysterious the region of Sheol was to Job he looks forward to it as a place in which, or from which, he could be, and he ventured to hope would be, called into conscious relation to the Holy One, and where the righteous man would have some light cast upon the unsolved problems of this strange life. The difference between the attitude of Job and that of his friends to death is therefore profoundly significant, and we can see clearly that he is leaving them far behind in development of soul and spiritual vision. He is concerned about far higher things than temporal prosperity.

He does not pray for death as a mere materialist, to whom death is the refuge of nonentity. To Job death is not only a negative but also a positive good. It is not merely a deliverance from pain and mystery, but also a means of closer access to the Holy One, who is the life of his life. In similar circumstances, when the body has been reduced to a mere wreck, when physical pain is extreme, and when nothing is left to hope for in this life, surely then, even to the most devout souls, the boon of death may become a legitimate object of prayer. "He giveth it to His beloved in sleep." To the man who has lived for the pleasures of sin during the brief season of this little life, and who has never even tried to love God as the Holy One, the approach of death may well be invested with terrors most appalling, even although it draw near amid such agonies that life is also terrible. Such a man may not pray for death with the awful judgment seat behind death, whereon sits the Holy One as the Judge of his unholy life.

But it is far otherwise with the man who can say amid the distresses which often accompany ap-

JOB'S EXPOSTULATIONS WITH GOD 197

proaching dissolution, "I have not denied the words of the Holy One." Death to him is deliverance, rest, interpretation, ascension. It is the last watch of the dreary night as the day begins to break and the shadows to flee away. It is the shady portal that leads into the near presence of the trusted Holy One, and opens out into regions of unknown light and peace. The near approach of death tests life as nothing else does. Blessed is the man who, like Job, can pray for the quickening of his lingering footsteps when he is near, thinking of his coming with no terror, but rather with a solemn gladness of anticipation as the messenger of God who comes to strike off the chains of his flesh that the free soul may rise into a fuller communion with its Redeemer. This is the man whose life is right in the sight of God, however it may be misjudged by his friends.

But we have now to note further that in his expostulations with God, Job bitterly and repeatedly complains that he receives no answer to any of his prayers, even to his prayers for death. God still remains silent after all his pleading, and his case continues to be still enveloped in inexplicable mystery. This silence and mystery on the part of God is terrible, and even unbearable, to Job. He cries out against it passionately again and again. "Shew me wherefore Thou contendest with me." "Wherefore hidest Thou thy face and holdest me for thine enemy?" "I cry unto Thee, and Thou dost not answer me: I stand up, and Thou lookest at me." Job admits that he himself can give no adequate explanation of his case. As for the explanations which his friends offer, he finds that they are mere "ashes." They are both futile and cruel: and they are not only unjust to him, but they are unjust to God also. God alone, he feels, can give the true explanation; but God has put him in the pillory of misery, and He looks upon his sufferings there, and listens to his cries of agony in a strange unresponsive silence. This is for Job his "sorrow's crown of sorrow." This is why, after his expostulations with God, and his flashes of faith, he again and again sinks back into those melancholy lamentations in which he sometimes comes near to utter despair.

Now it is well for us to note that this profound sadness in trial is not peculiar to Job, but common among Old Testament saints; and that we should further note the striking contrast between the attitude and tone of Old Testament saints in trial and suffering and the attitude and tone of New

JOB'S EXPOSTULATIONS WITH GOD 199

Testament saints in like circumstances. It is the difference between an autumn evening and a summer morning. We see that when the Old Testament saint is face to face with life's most awful trials it is with the utmost difficulty that he holds on to his faith at all, and that, as with Job, there is always a deep wail in or near his expressions of faith. Even in Job's great burst of faith, recorded in the nineteenth chapter, his grand prophecy of immortality and final vindication has a long preface full of saddest lament, and immediately after it he sinks back to the same lamentations again.

But look at the marvellous hopefulness and buoyancy, and even joyousness, of the New Testament saints amid all their fearful sufferings! Jesus said to His disciples—" Blessed are ye when men shall reproach you and persecute you, and say all manner of evil against you falsely, for my sake. Rejoice, and be exceeding glad, for great is your reward in heaven." And His disciples responded in a wonderful way to this wonderful call to rejoice in suffering. They fixed the vision of their faith upon the after glory and upon the ascended Son of Man. They said—
" Our light affliction, which is but for a moment, worketh for us a far more exceeding, even an

eternal weight of glory, while we look, not at the things that are seen, but at the things that are not seen ; for the things that are seen are temporal, but the things that are not seen are eternal."

Stephen could be stoned with the face of an angel, because he endured as seeing Him who is invisible. Paul and Silas could sing with their feet fast in the stocks, because their souls were free to hold communion with the unseen Christ. John, a prisoner in a Roman convict settlement in a lonely island, could rise to such an ecstasy of soul in his communion with heaven as no words can express. Peter tells us that he and his fellow-disciples, being put to grief in manifold temptations, yet believing, rejoiced with joy unspeakable and full of glory. James counted it all joy when he fell into divers trials, and urged his brethren to do the same. Paul can write that wonderful catalogue of his sufferings and put a balancing word over against each word that records the different phases of his daily martyrdom. He is persecuted, but not forsaken ; he is cast down, but not destroyed. He can glory in his affliction. He says—" I take pleasure in infirmities, in reproaches, in necessities, in per-

JOB'S EXPOSTULATIONS WITH GOD 201

secutions, in distresses, for Christ's sake." We find the same spirit common among the Christian martyrs from the very first.

Now what is the explanation of this most remarkable contrast between the conduct of the Old Testament saints and that of the New Testament saints under severe trial? The answer lies in the one supreme fact—Christ has come, and has brought life and immortality to light. And Christian men and women should never forget that they belong to New Testament, and not to Old Testament times. It is not enough— it is not worthy of our great privileges—that we should follow Job in the days of our great trials, but we must follow Paul.

But the most striking parts of Job's expostulations with God are those in which he deals with his own sin. He knows that the moral problem is the deepest aspect of his case, and so he comes at last to personal guilt as the root question in relation to all his misery.

Now there are four distinct steps in his thought here. His first thought is that if he has sinned he cannot see how such a Being as God should be affected by the sin of such a creature as himself. " If I have sinned, what do I unto Thee, O Thou watcher of men?" His next thought is that, judging by the rewards and punishments of God's providence, he is unable to distinguish between the righteous and the wicked, or to see any sure advantage in being righteous—" If I sin, then Thou markest me, and Thou wilt not acquit me from mine iniquity. If I be wicked, woe unto me; and if I be righteous yet shall I not lift up my head; being filled with ignominy and looking upon mine affliction." His third thought is that seeing that it is impossible for any man to rid himself of his own guilt or to right himself before God, therefore it is wonderful that God should deal with him in such severity. "Dost Thou open Thine eyes upon such an one, and bringest me into judgment with Thee? Who can bring a clean thing out of an unclean? Not one." Job's final thought in this connection is the most striking of all. He wonders why, seeing that the case of man stands thus, God does not Himself come to the rescue of His helpless creature and deal with his sin in such a way as will restore the purity of his nature and bring him back to happiness and peace. "Why doest Thou not pardon my transgression, and take away mine iniquity?" he asks. It is here,

JOB'S EXPOSTULATIONS WITH GOD 203

perhaps, more than anywhere, that the remarkable spiritual penetration of this ancient Hebrew poet is revealed.

When Job says, " If I have sinned "—the " if," which is several times repeated, is an illuminative word for the whole book. For a man so prosperous as Job had been the great temptation in that day was for him to think very little of his sin and much of his righteousness. Job did, indeed, need to maintain his integrity as against the false theory of his friends; but he had no ground for maintaining it in any absolute sense against conscience and against God. He does not sufficiently realise at first that his innocence was only relative. It is plain from his questioning confession that he is far enough from being able to speak of himself as Paul does of himself in the seventh chapter of his letter to the Romans, or as Augustine wrote of himself in his " Confessions," or as Bunyan wrote of himself in his " Grace abounding to the Chief of Sinners."

This question lets us into the secret and necessity of Job's trial from his side, and it prepares us for the condemnation of his self-justification afterwards given by the great Voice out of the storm. Job takes away the " if " at last; and as soon as he "abhors himself in dust and ashes" in the sight and presence of God his salvation has come. But at first he is so far from having reached this state that he asks if he has sinned, how that can affect God. "If I have sinned, what do I unto Thee, O Thou watcher of men?" God is here for the moment viewed as a great detective, for ever watching to catch His creature in a fault.

Job's tendency here is to think of God's greatness as removing Him far above the region in which the sin of such an insignificant creature as himself can trouble Him. But here the conception which Job has of the moral relations between God and man is far below the truth; for all God's dealings with men, and all His revelations to men tend to convince us that He is affected, and profoundly affected, by our sin. Job did not yet see this; for the influence of the false theory which he was combating, almost unconsciously led him astray as he noted that the righteous often fared no better than the wicked in the world.

But if he was wrong in the first two points how profoundly right he was in the last two, although there is almost a kind of irreverent

JOB'S EXPOSTULATIONS WITH GOD 205

audacity in the way he utters his thought. " Why dost Thou not pardon my transgression and take away my sin ? " How relevant is that question to the redemption afterwards achieved ? Why, indeed, if God be such as He is—such a God as Christ has revealed Him to be—why should He not both pardon and cleanse the sinner, even at that awful cost at which alone this was possible ? This indeed would be unlike man ; but then it would be all the more like God for that. Job did not know at what a cost that pardon could alone be obtained. He did not apprehend the deep relations of these questions of his to the divine character, in justice as well as in love and mercy. Therefore God had to reprove him for darkening counsel with words without knowledge.

Yet Job was deeply, mainly right in looking steadfastly to the one source from which alone any true help could come. And how wonderfully has his great double question been answered since in the redemptive sacrifice of Christ and the spiritual development of men. Some may feel shocked at the exceeding boldness of Job's language ; but if we are to choose between frank and even bold questioning about the strange facts of life, and pious conventional cant, which may not be wholly hypocritical, but which nevertheless plays with words for the sake of a transient spiritual ease—then we know from the authoritative verdict in the epilogue which God Himself prefers. "Ye have not spoken of *Me* the thing that is right, as my servant Job hath." The pronoun here is very noteworthy. It is the way the friends have spoken of God, not of Job, that is condemned.

If we have our questions of the heart and of the soul, let us come and state them frankly and honestly and earnestly, and yet with becoming humility in the ear of God, that He may enable us to understand, that we may see our need and sin to be as deep and great as they really are, and also that we may see God's love and mercy to be enough for all our need, and so by His prevailing grace rise from our own deep darkness into His marvellous light. Then when we ask this great question for ourselves—" Why dost Thou not pardon my transgression, and take away mine iniquity ?" we, too, shall hear the divine Voice, but speaking to us out of the great storm of the divine passion—speaking far more wonderfully to us than ever it did to Job—

JOB'S EXPOSTULATIONS WITH GOD 207

and saying—"God so loved the world, that He gave His only begotten Son, that whosoever believeth on Him should not perish, but have eternal life." "The Son of Man came not to be ministered unto, but to minister, and to give His life a ransom for many."

CHAPTER IX

THE INTERVENTION OF ELIHU

AT the close of the final speech of Job a new character is introduced who is described as " Elihu, the son of Barachel the Buzite, of the family of Ram." His contribution to the discussion occupies no fewer than six chapters of the book, and is in many ways important. It may be viewed as one prolonged speech, as there is no interruption to his discourse ; or it may be regarded as four successive speeches, with three pauses between the parts to give Job opportunities for answering the arguments urged against him, if he has anything to say. Job, however, remains silent.

The connecting link between the last speech of Job and the speech of Elihu is furnished by five prose verses, in which the poet speaks in his own person, and explains the cause and purpose of Elihu's intervention. He is a young man of a devout and reverent spirit, and as a bystander

THE INTERVENTION OF ELIHU 209

he has been listening to the whole debate with the most intense interest. As he listened he grew more and more angry with Job; because he seemed to be more concerned about justifying himself before God than about justifying the ways of God with men, as if the justification of God were less important than his own. This was an attitude which Elihu regarded as the most shocking impiety.

But Elihu's anger blazed out in two opposite directions; for he was angry at Job's three friends as well; because, on the one hand, they had handled their good case so badly that they had allowed Job to silence them; and yet, on the other hand, they had not therefore admitted Job to be in the right, but had condemned him all the same, as if they had themselves been victors in the debate. The one purpose, therefore, for which Elihu intervenes in the discussion is to justify the ways of God in His providence; and this he proposes to do by showing that both Job and his friends are in the wrong; he, because he suffers himself to be ruled by an impious spirit; they, because while their intentions are good, they err through incapacity, which leads them to argue in a wrong way for God, and also

o

to treat Job somewhat unfairly. It is, however, with Job that his main business lies; and while his whole speech is intended to be an implicit rebuke to the three friends as showing them how they should have handled the case against Job, he does not, after the first part of his speech, return to deal in a direct manner any further with their errors.

Who, then, is Elihu, and what relation does his contribution bear to the rest of the book? Here the question of the integrity of the book is raised in a more serious form than that in which we found it was raised in connection with the last speech of Job. So great an authority as Lightfoot suggested that Elihu might be the author of the whole book. But this is, for many reasons, in a high degree improbable, especially because he does not deal with the main problem raised, in view of the situations revealed in the prologue and epilogue, at all.

Some modern critics have allowed themselves great freedom in discussing the integrity of the book. Some hold that the fortieth and forty-first chapters are also interpolated as well as the speeches of Elihu. Others regard the prologue and epilogue as being together fragments of an

THE INTERVENTION OF ELIHU 211

earlier work. Some would also cut out the speeches of Jehovah altogether; while Cheyne seems to persuade himself that the book consists of no fewer than four distinct parts which were probably originally distinct, namely, a prose work consisting of the prologue and epilogue, the debate between Job and his friends, the speeches of Jehovah, and the speeches of Elihu. Most of these speculations are too fanciful to require serious answers. At any rate, it will be enough to deal here with the difficulty presented in relation to the speeches of Elihu alone. No fewer than eight reasons have been given for regarding these as the work of a later author.

I. Elihu is not mentioned either in the prologue or in the epilogue. It must, however, be remembered not only that Elihu is merely a bystander, and does not rank as a friend of Job, but that he is a severe critic of the friends of Job as well as of Job himself. Still, he makes an important contribution to the discussion, and therefore it is not easy to answer the question: Why is he wholly ignored in the epilogue? It is, indeed, said that the epilogue is very brief, and that the arguments of Elihu are very similar to those of the friends; but the difficulty raised is not fully met by such rejoinders.

II. No reply is given to Elihu, either by Job, or by the Voice out of the storm. But with regard to Job, it was clearly the intention of the author to represent Job as silenced by the arguments of Elihu, even as the friends were silenced by those of Job, and the silence is as reasonable in the one case as in the other. But the reference to the silence of Jehovah is quite a different matter. As the speech of Jehovah follows immediately after that of Elihu, it would have seemed most natural that some reference should have been made to some of Elihu's sayings by the divine Voice. On the other hand, we should remember that the arguments of the friends receive no more attention from God than those of Elihu, and that while He answers Job He does not do so by meeting his arguments in detail.

III. Elihu quotes the speeches of Job with such minuteness as to suggest that he is quoting as the reader of a book rather than as a listener from memory. There is some truth in this contention; but how little bearing it has on the main question is seen from the fact that Dr Watson, who is confident that the speeches of

THE INTERVENTION OF ELIHU 213

Elihu are not only the work of a later author but of one so late as the exile, has to admit that Elihu not only misquotes Job on several main points, but that he sometimes does so in such a way as to quite reverse his meaning.

IV. It is said that the intervention of Elihu destroys the natural connection between the last speech of Job and the first part of the divine speech. One cannot but feel that there is some force in this argument. And yet remarkably diverse views have been taken with regard to it by equally competent critics. For while Dr Davidson thinks that the first part of the divine speech would naturally follow immediately after the speech of Job, Godet, on the other hand, holds that the speech of Elihu forms a connection between the two which is not only beautiful, but in some respects necessary to the completeness of the book as a whole.

V. It is further held that the style and language of the speeches of Elihu indicate that they are the work of a later author. On this point Dr Davidson says—" The speeches of Elihu are marked by a deeper colouring of Aramaic ; are frequently very obscure ; and not seldom descend almost to the level of prose. The touches of

214 AFFLICTIONS OF THE RIGHTEOUS

the author's hand in the other parts of the poem, particularly in the divine speeches, are easy, vigorous, and graphic ; in the speeches of Elihu the figures are laboured, and the thought strained." M. Renan agrees that the speeches of Elihu are inferior to the rest of the work. He says—" In the other parts of the poem the obscurity arises from our own ignorance ; here it arises from the style itself." But this does not altogether convince M. Renan that this part of the book must be by another author, for he suggests that it may have been added by the same author at a later period when his powers had begun to decline.

It has been also suggested that the difficulty might be met by referring it to the dramatic genius of the author, to which suggestion Dr Davidson makes a reply that has a fine flavour of genuine Scottish humour in it. He says that this is "to ascribe to the author a proficiency in the dramatic art scarcely probable in his age, to imagine that he makes Elihu talk Aramean, as Shakespeare makes Captain Jamy talk something supposed to be Scotch. If this were the case, however, the older dramatist would appear to have the advantage of the modern one." Yet

THE INTERVENTION OF ELIHU 215

we cannot allow this argument about the inferiority of the speeches of Elihu to carry us too far; for not only is it reasonable to suppose that in these the poet was reserving his full powers in order that he might make the great speech of Jehovah as worthy of the divine Speaker as possible; but besides, the latter part of the speech of Elihu reaches so high a level of poetic art, that it has attracted the special admiration of the most competent critics.

Indeed Dr Watson feels the force of this fact so much that he is constrained to account for it by suggesting that this latter part of Elihu's speech must be the work of a third author, a man of much greater genius than that of the post-exilic poet. "There need be little hesitation," he says, "in regarding this passage as an ode supplied to the second writer, or simply quoted by him, for the purpose of giving strength to his argument."

VI. It is further said that Elihu covers the same ground which has been gone over by the three friends. Dr Davidson thinks that this objection has considerable force. He says—" A fourth speaker would be introduced only if he had to occupy ground entirely distinct from the other three. And it cannot be said that Elihu does so." The answer to this is twofold. First, the same argument would lead to the elimination, if not of both Bildad and Zophar, certainly of Zophar from the debate; for undoubtedly Elihu has at least as much to contribute of original matter to the discussion as either of these. But besides, is it not clear that, *whoever* the author of Elihu's speeches was, *he* thought that in these a new and important contribution was made to the discussion of the subject ? If they were mere repetition would there not obviously be not more but less reason for a subsequent than for the original author to introduce them ?

VII. Another ground for questioning the integrity of the book is that there is a theological diversity between the speeches of Elihu and the other parts of it. This argument seems to be so weak as to merit, very little notice; for however Elihu's conception of God may differ from that of the other speakers, the same is true of Job's conception of God, in comparison to that of the others, only to a much greater degree. Moreover, this would militate against the preceding point as being an important reason for introducing Elihu.

THE INTERVENTION OF ELIHU 217

VIII. A final argument in favour of composite authorship is that the whole section containing the speeches of Elihu could be removed without affecting the other parts of the book in any way. This is not quite accurate, because the removal of Elihu's speeches would indirectly affect the other parts of the book. Besides, so far as it it true, the argument proves too much; because other parts of the book could be removed also, leaving the remainder with the appearance of being unmutilated in the same way.

Some of the chief arguments in favour of the integrity of the book are—

I. If the speeches of Elihu had been the work of a later author who had the whole book in his hand, he would not have ignored the contents of the prologue and the epilogue. This seems to be a strong argument, and one not easily met.

II. Elihu's speeches form an important element in the organic unity of the book. His wisdom is designed to contrast with the spurious wisdom of the friends, and his reverence to contrast with the rashness of Job. But one may have some doubt as to whether the wisdom of Elihu is greatly superior to that of Eliphaz.

III. Elihu is intended by the original author

to be a caricature of the three friends. This is a remarkably weak argument. Certainly there are some things in the manner in which Elihu introduces himself which offend against good taste; but to use these to form a theory like this is to exaggerate them beyond all reason.

IV. The speeches of Elihu are an important part of the original design of the book, because they form a necessary transition stage between the close of the debate and the parts that follow them. The first two speeches of Elihu are said to prepare the way for Job's submission, and the last two for the answer of the Voice out of the storm, so that they thus form an important point of double transition. This argument has considerable force, and it is impressively handled by Godet. He says—" Nothing is abler, better managed, and in some respects more indispensable, psychologically speaking, than this intermediate part, as the gentle exhortation of Elihu forms the transition from the hard words of the friends to the solemn revelation, so does the silence of Job before Elihu form the transition between his haughty answers to his friends, and his humble and complete self-humiliation before Jehovah." But, as we shall see, some of the words which

Elihu addresses to Job are not quite accurately described as " gentle exhortation."

V. Most scholars who argue for composite authorship give to the book an exilic or post-exilic date; and they give the Elihu speeches in particular a later date than the Hebrew oracles on the suffering Servant. But in that case it would be quite inexplicable that there should be no reference whatever in the Elihu speeches to the profound explanation of Job's problem suggested by the idea of vicarious suffering in these oracles. Professor Peake frankly admits the great force of this argument.

On the whole, it can hardly be said that a case either for or against the integrity of the book has been conclusively proved. It is true that the majority of modern critics are in favour of the theory that the speeches of Elihu are the work of a later author; but the most that can be said for that theory is that it has the balance of probability in its favour.

Elihu opens his first speech with a somewhat elaborate apology for his intervention. This apology at once reveals a remarkable combination of devout humility and egotistical pretension in his character. He shows that he is not without the modesty proper to youth in presence of men who are "very old." That was why he had listened so long in silence to the poor arguments of the friends. Men of such great experience, he felt, *ought* to be wiser than he; and so he had hoped against hope that their arguments would mend. Instead of that they only went from bad to worse, until they made him quite angry. Then he began to feel some confidence in his own ability in contrast to such a poor display. He declares that he has listened with the closest attention to all that the three friends had to say; but although he is strongly on the side for which they have been trying to argue he feels bound to confess that none of them gave such an answer to Job as might reasonably be expected to convince him that they were in the right and he was in the wrong. He pictures the friends as being "amazed" at the extraordinary ability with which Job has confuted their arguments; but he rejects with impatience the idea that Job is so formidable an antagonist that only "God may vanquish him, not man."

He suggests rather that their failure in the debate is due to their own incapacity, and not to any extraordinary genius on the part of Job

THE INTERVENTION OF ELIHU 221

in managing a bad case. This being the situation Elihu asks what ought now to be done. Should the just cause of God be publicly abandoned because three incompetent men have so completely failed to treat it worthily ? Elihu feels that there is only one answer possible to that question. Therefore he is prepared to lay aside his natural modesty, and come forward himself as the champion of God for whom the occasion so urgently calls.

He claims to be conscious of a divine inspiration in addressing himself to this task, and therefore he attempts it with strong confidence. He pledges himself that his arguments against Job will be original : " For he hath not directed his words against me ; neither will I answer him with your speeches." " I also will answer my part ; I also will show my opinion. For I am full of words ; the spirit within me constraineth me." He promises also to conduct the discussion with frankness and fairness, and without flattery in any direction.

The general effect of this introductory passage is to make us feel that Elihu is very kind to himself and rather hard on the friends. He enters into the lists with a very considerable flourish of trumpets, and raises within us very high expectations as to the part he is going to play and how he is going to play it. But when we have carefully compared his speeches with those of the friends, we have more than a suspicion that he has not altogether fulfilled the hopes he thus created.

At the beginning of the thirty-third chapter, Elihu turns from the friends and addresses himself directly to Job. He begins by making new protestations concerning his own uprightness and sincerity, and he repeats his claim to a kind of divine inspiration in conducting this argument. He urges Job to knit himself together, and to stand up like a man and do his best to answer the case against him as he is now going to state it, thus suggesting that Job's task in dealing with him will be a very different affair from his experience in answering the three friends.

Job had complained that the greatness of God overawed him and had desired a daysman. Elihu now puts himself forth in that capacity; for while he comes to Job with a new and inspired wisdom, yet he is on the same human plane with Job. "I also am formed out of clay," he says. "Behold, my terror shall not make thee afraid, neither

THE INTERVENTION OF ELIHU

shall my pressure be heavy upon thee." But alas! the qualifications of Elihu, with all his virtues, to take the part of daysman, as Job conceived it and felt the need of it, are only too plainly lacking, and that both on the human and on the divine side.

After these somewhat portentous preliminaries Elihu selects a central, and to his mind most offensive point in Job's argument as the object of his first attack. Job had complained that God subjected him to mysterious sufferings for which he could see no adequate cause, yet when he appealed to God for some explanation He gave him no answer. He quotes Job as saying—" I am clean; without transgression; I am innocent, neither is there iniquity in me." But the way in which he thus overstates Job's claim to innocence shows that Elihu is no nearer a true understanding of Job's contention than any of the three friends.

Elihu's reply to this complaint of Job is— First, that God is not responsible to anyone for the way in which He chooses to govern His world. " For God is greater than man. Why dost thou strive against Him ? For He giveth not account of any of His matters." Elihu here shows himself incapable of rising to the lofty conception which Job had of the spiritual relation between the Creator and His moral creatures. He passes lightly over this; but he deals more worthily with Job's complaint about the inaccessibility of God. He meets it with a direct negative, and specifies three ways in which God communicates with man. The first way is by dream or vision. Obviously all dreams cannot be regarded as means of divine communication. But Elihu's contention is justified if it can be shown that some dreams are. The second way is by chastisement in affliction. He does not here expressly say that this is Job's case; but the description which he gives of a man in a wasting disease suggests that he has him in his mind. The third way in which God communicates His mind to men is by means of a messenger, who is a mediator or interpreter, who is able to show the perplexed man what is right. Probably Elihu here had present to his mind himself, and the part which he was now playing in relation to Job.

It is noteworthy that Elihu emphasises the fact that the divine purpose in all these three ways of communicating with men is the same, namely, that the sinner may be delivered and

THE INTERVENTION OF ELIHU 225

restored. Here he introduces his distinctly original and most interesting idea of a divine ransom as the means for the accomplishment of this purpose. What precisely the ransom is he leaves in obscurity; but two points in connection with it he makes quite clear. The first is that it is provided by God, and not by the sinner. In his second reference to the ransom in a subsequent speech he makes this plainer still by declaring that nothing that Job could furnish could be regarded as an adequate ransom by God.

The second point is that the ransom is provided for the sinner by God on the ground of his confession and repentance. "Then he singeth before men, and saith—I have sinned and perverted that which was right, and it profited me not: He hath redeemed my soul from going into the pit." At the conclusion of this part of his argument Elihu challenges Job to reply to him if he feels able to do so—" If thou hast anything to say, answer me: Speak, for I desire to justify thee. If not, hearken thou unto me: hold thy peace, and I will teach thee wisdom." But Job remains silent, and so Elihu proceeds to the next part of his discourse.

This part is addressed, not to Job, but to the
P

"wise men," that is, all the bystanders who are capable of forming a judgment on the matter, the discussion being regarded as a public debate which had attracted much attention. He turns from the silent Job to them as to umpires in the case, as being willing to abide by their verdict, as if he should say, "I speak as unto wise men, judge ye what I say." In this section of his discourse Elihu deals with another selected saying of Job, namely, that God afflicted him with incurable wounds while he was " without transgression." He mentions here another saying of Job's that it is no profit for a man to be religious, but he reserves it as the text of a direct address to Job in the next chapter.

Elihu begins his argument to the wise men with a severe attack on Job, in which he accuses him of absolute wickedness and of being a companion of wicked men. " What man is like Job, who drinketh up scorning like water? Who goeth in company with the workers of iniquity, and walketh with wicked men." Here again Elihu shows a serious lack of true discernment; and indeed he cannot be exonerated from a charge of unfairness, despite all his preliminary protestations, in working up his case against

THE INTERVENTION OF ELIHU 227

Job. For whatever Job might be accused of it was simply absurd to class a man with a record like his with the very worst of men; and besides, even in his rashest utterances, Job had clearly showed that he was a man of earnest spiritual life. It was the very intensity of his earnestness as a religious man which made him speak as he did; and men who were incapable of perceiving this were not qualified to judge his case at all.

Elihu, however, is full of a genuine religious horror at Job's assertion that God is unjust, and he lays it down as a fundamental general principle that this is utterly impossible in the very nature of things. God, he points out, does not rule with any delegated authority, but as the Almighty, the Creator and Sustainer of all things. Such a Ruler must rule in righteousness, for He has no motive for ruling otherwise. What could He be supposed to gain by ruling unjustly? Who could bribe Him, or who would reward him for acting otherwise than according to His desire? " Yea, of a surety, God will not do wickedly, neither will the Almighty pervert judgment. Who gave Him a charge over the whole earth? Or who hath disposed the whole world?"

Elihu further goes on to show that this righteous rule of God is grounded upon God's omniscience and omnipotence. "For His eyes are upon the ways of a man, and He seeth all his goings. There is no darkness nor shadow of death where the workers of iniquity may hide themselves." And if no evil man can hide any of his evil from God, neither can any resist Him in the execution of the judgment which he knows, from all the facts which are open to him alone, to be absolutely just. "He breaketh in pieces mighty men in ways past finding out, and setteth others in their stead." Elihu's final point in this connection is that it is unreasonable for any man to complain against the judgment of God because there is no one higher than He to whom appeal might be made against it. "When He giveth quietness, who then can condemn? And when He hideth His face, who then can behold Him? Whether it be done unto a nation, or unto a man, alike."

Elihu concludes therefore that the judgments of God should be accepted with humility. But he appeals to the wise men to consider how far otherwise it has been with Job; and so he ex- expresses a harsh desire to see Job tried unto

THE INTERVENTION OF ELIHU 229

the end—" Because of his answering like wicked men. For he addeth rebellion to his sin." In this appeal to the wise Elihu repeatedly asserts that the wicked are punished and the righteous delivered as actual facts in the providence of God, just as the three friends had done. But the very point of Job's difficulty was that often this was not so, and this was burned into him by his own experience. This is the very heart of Job's problem, and Elihu leaves it unanswered still.

At the beginning of the thirty-fifth chapter Elihu turns from the wise men and resumes his direct attack on Job, this time on the ground of his complaint that it was no profit for a man to be religious. His first answer to this is that God is so great that Job's goodness or badness matters nothing to him, though it might be of some consequence to other men around him. " If thou be righteous, what givest thou unto Him ? Or what receiveth He of thine hand ? Thy wickedness may hurt a man as thou art ; and thy righteousness may profit a son of man." Now we have already seen this was the very view that Job himself took when he said—" If I have sinned, what do I unto thee, O Thou Watcher

230 AFFLICTIONS OF THE RIGHTEOUS

of men ? " He found no comfort in it, but used it as an argument why God should at least let him alone. But the truth is, as we saw, that this is a wrong view of the relation between God and men, and that God is affected, and profoundly affected by the conduct of men.

Elihu's second answer to this complaint of Job is that Men when in trouble often cry out much as the beasts do in pain, but their cry does not mean that they recognise God's hand in their trouble, nor consider that it comes from Him who "giveth songs in the night," and whose purpose is to teach us by means of the trouble more than the beasts know. Such prayers, Elihu says, God answers not, because they are the offspring of vanity and pride. Now, whatever value there may be in these observations as general statements, we feel that they are quite irrelevant as applied to Job. For all along he most clearly recognises the hand of God in his affliction, and indeed that is, as we have seen, the chief reason why it is so mysterious and terrible to him.

Elihu's third answer to this complaint is that although a man may not be able to see that things are working out for his good, that is no proof that

THE INTERVENTION OF ELIHU 231

they are not actually doing so; but it is a reason why he should trust in God beyond his understanding of the way by which God is leading him. " Although thou sayest thou beholdest Him not, yet judgment is before Him; therefore trust thou in Him." This was an exhortation which Job needed; and it is one which men in trouble very often need. Elihu suggests that Job might have been expected to learn this lesson of trust in God from the extreme nature of his own trials; but he has not done so, and therefore his words are both foolish and vain. Here Elihu makes another pause, but as Job continues silent he proceeds with the final part of his discourse.

In all his previous speeches Elihu, as we have seen, has been engaged in combating what he considered Job's false views of God and His ways. But in this, his final and longest speech, which occupies two entire chapters, he forsakes his method of destructive criticism, and becomes a positive teacher, seeking to set forth in contrast to Job's false ideas his own true picture of God and His ways with men. Elihu introduces this part of his teaching in a passage which is richly flavoured with that egotism and pretentiousness which we have already noted as peculiar to him. "I will fetch my knowledge from far, and will ascribe righteousness to my Maker. For truly my words are not false: one that is perfect in knowledge is with thee." We could not have greatly wondered if at this point Job had broken his silence to repeat his former saying: "No doubt but you are the man, and wisdom will die with you." What follows, however, is really the finest and the most important part of Elihu's contribution to the discussion.

He begins by showing that God's power is wonderful not by the mere magnitude of it as irresistible force, but because it is wise and moral and gracious. He rules over all with such perfect justice that all get their deserts, whether they are good or bad. But the justice of God is a wise and considerate justice, which deals graciously with the weak and the lowly. "Behold God is mighty, and despiseth not any: He is mighty in strength of understanding."

Then Elihu goes on to develop his theory of suffering as being on God's part a gracious discipline which reveals, to those who can appreciate it rightly, a special phase of the divine goodness. "If they be bound in fetters, and be taken

THE INTERVENTION OF ELIHU 233

in the cords of affliction, then He showeth them their work, and their transgressions, that they have behaved themselves proudly. He openeth also their ear to instruction, and commandeth that they return from iniquity." God's design in all this is to restore the sinner to happiness, but it is notable that Elihu's idea of the *summum bonum* is as it was in the teaching of the three friends, expressed in terms of temporal prosperity. "They shall spend their days in prosperity, and their years in pleasures." What shall be the result of such discipline to each man who is subjected to it will depend entirely, says Elihu, upon how the man receives it. If he repents, deliverance and blessing shall follow, if not, disaster and death.

Now as a general theory of Providence this is excellent; but Elihu immediately proceeds to make a most pointed application of these principles to the case of Job with the intention of proving, just as the three friends had tried to do, that Job is a remarkably wicked man. He lays it down as an axiom that in Job's case too it was the intention of God to lead him through affliction to a higher, purer life, and to richer, fuller blessing, and then he *assumes* that the only reason why Job continues in his present state of utter wretchedness is that he is proud and self-righteous and still cherishes iniquity in his heart; and so he says to him plainly— "Thou art full of the judgment of the wicked: judgment and justice take hold on thee." He therefore exhorts Job earnestly, and quite sincerely, to turn from his iniquity lest worse things still befall him through the increasing anger of God. Here again Elihu's remarkable idea of a "ransom" reappears, and he emphatically declares that all Job's riches and all that he can offer will not be regarded by God as an adequate ransom to deliver him from the just judgment due to his sins. His only hope is in the mercy of God, and this is only to be obtained by genuine repentance.

At this point the speech of Elihu finds wings and rises to a wonderful poetic flight, far above the level of his previous utterances. His theme is the greatness of God, in wisdom and in power, as exhibited in his works. The passage is largely descriptive of natural phenomena: the language employed is exquisitely beautiful and admirably adapted to its purpose: the imagery and analogies are most skilfully chosen, and are managed with a consummate poetic art which is sustained to the very close of the speech.

All this great effort is directed to impress three important facts deeply upon the mind of Job. The first is that God is so exceeding great that it is impossible for such creatures as men to understand him: "Behold, God is great, and we know Him not." The second fact, is that the works of God are also so great and marvellous that they, as well as He, transcend the apprehension of the human mind: "Great things doeth He, which we cannot comprehend." The third fact is that man is nevertheless gifted with such powers that he is able to understand the works of God sufficiently to be profoundly impressed by them so that the contemplation of them is fitted to bring him into a proper state of reverence and humility in presence of such a Being as their Author. Therefore Elihu calls upon Job to—"Stand still, and consider the wondrous works of God."

Elihu is persuaded that if Job will only earnestly consider these works he cannot fail to be humbled in the dust; and there is a touch of irony in the questions which he hurls one after another at Job in this connection—"Dost thou know the balancing of the clouds, the wondrous works of Him which is perfect in knowledge?" "Canst thou with him spread out the sky, which is strong as a molten mirror? Teach us what we shall say unto him; for we cannot order our speech by reason of darkness." Elihu feels that for himself he has no words wherewith to contend with so august a Being. He is afraid that if he should attempt to do so he would be "swallowed up." His final conclusion, therefore, is that men, and Job in particular, should never dream of judging or criticising such a Being. They should rather be filled with fear and awe in presence of His "terrible majesty"; for "He regardeth not any that are wise of heart," that is, who are wise in their "inner light," or in their own conceit.

Viewing the speeches of Elihu as a whole we find that they reveal him as a person with certain characteristics of egotism and pretentiousness, which, if they are not altogether offensive, yet do not commend him to us as being a man in all respects qualified to fulfil successfully the difficult part which he has undertaken. On the whole he is gentler and fairer towards Job than the three

THE INTERVENTION OF ELIHU 237

friends were, especially during the latter part of the debate ; and yet, as I have already pointed out, there are certain passages in his discourse which are characterised by a singular harshness and severity.

It is notable also that Elihu does not attempt to deal with Job's case with any breadth or comprehensiveness of view, nor set himself to grapple with the central problem involved in anything like the way which Job had endeavoured to do. His method rather is to select certain isolated sayings of Job which seemed most readily exposed to his attack, and to make the most of his case by cleverly controverting these. This is a method which may be commended for its astuteness and sagacity if the end in view is merely a personal triumph in debate, but it has not so much to commend it to the mind whose chief object is the discovery of the truth. It can hardly be said, however, that even Elihu's special examinations of his selected sayings of Job are adequate, notwithstanding all their ability ; for as we have repeatedly seen, he often misstates Job's position in such a way as to give himself a decided advantage in the discussion of it, so that his real success is often not so great as it appears to be.

Another outstanding feature of Elihu's method in conducting his argument is the way in which he deals so largely in generalities as to obscure the real nature of the issues. And in this respect he once more reminds us of the way in which the three friends had treated Job. He ignores the specific facts which Job had set forth as being hopelessly opposed to the orthodox theory of Providence, and instead of dealing with these he envelopes the difficulties of the suffering saint in clouds of words, which describe, sometimes with great beauty and impressiveness, the general lines of a more or less imaginery moral order, but which leave the very crux of Job's personal problem completely untouched.

But perhaps the most serious of the defects in the speeches of Elihu is the way in which he sometimes condescends to browbeat Job when he is hard pressed to find some worthier method of argument. He tells Job that God is so great that Job is a mere thing of no consequence whatever to Him. God could do this, that, and the other thing to Job, and what could Job do in the way of resisting God? God could blow Job

THE INTERVENTION OF ELIHU

into utter oblivion by a mere breath. Job therefore should be very thankful to be allowed to live at all in presence of such a Being. In these passages there is an absurd predominance given to the element of mere power, and there is a singular lack of anything like a true appreciation of the moral and spiritual relationship which must of necessity exist between God and all His moral creatures. Such passages are strikingly at variance with the finer passages in the speeches of Job, and also with the teaching of both the prologue and the epilogue in reference to the same subject.

On the other hand, however, Elihu shows himself to be a man of a beautiful devoutness and earnestness of spirit. He has a most profound reverence for God, and he has a genuine desire to bring Job into the same worshipful attitude towards him. Although there are some things in him which we cannot help resenting, yet there are many other things about him also which render him attractive and command our respect. The religion of Elihu is neither formal nor superficial, but it is both deep and fervent, and indeed the very harshness with which he sometimes addresses Job may be regarded as springing from the intensity of his religious feeling. He is obviously sincere in making the supreme end of all his discourse the justification of the ways of God with men, and if in his endeavour to achieve this end he is sometimes less than just to Job that arises from no desire or intention on his part to be so, but rather from his failure to appreciate the full bearings of his own arguments upon the inner aspects of Job's case.

By far the most important original contribution which Elihu makes to the discussion is in connection with his theory of the causes and the function of human suffering. It is surely going too far to say with Dr Davidson that Elihu never speaks of suffering as purely penal and intended to destroy, for he has a good deal to say about the destruction of the wicked. But while the three friends regarded suffering as being always the result of sin done, Elihu teaches that God sometimes imposes suffering where no sin has been done, with the intention of saving a man from falling into sin towards which he is inclined, affliction in that case being preventive rather than redemptive or penal. Speaking generally Elihu's view of sin may be truly said to be more inward and more spiritual than that

THE INTERVENTION OF ELIHU 241

of the three friends ; but when we compare Elihu's view of sin to that of Job, we find that it is as much inferior to Job's view in depth and spirituality as it is superior in these respects to that of his friends.

But the most original and striking of all Elihu's ideas is that human suffering is generally to be regarded as the expression of God's goodness rather than of his anger. He teaches that sometimes it is not a sign of any anger in God at all, but rather a sign of his protective and educative love, protecting a man by a shield of pain from the greater evil of sin, and educating him to higher and purer levels of thought and desire that he may be able to hold deeper fellowship with Himself and so reach higher blessedness. There are many good things in Elihu's speeches, but this is the best of them all.

CHAPTER X

THE DIVINE INTERPRETATION

THIS speech of Jehovah is so great that it is only after we have studied it with care that we begin to perceive how great it really is. Any intelligent mind, even on a cursory reading of it, must be profoundly impressed by the magnificent display of poetic genius which it contains; for here this great world-poet brings all the resources of his wonderful art into their fullest exercise. But the very brilliance of the form in which the thought is set forth is apt to dazzle the mind of the reader, so that he may not readily perceive the real worth of the profound line of argument which runs through the whole speech. Certainly this crowning speech far surpasses, as it was intended to do, all that has hitherto been said in answer to Job; and it produces so great an effect upon him that he is led by it at last to such a deep repentance that he regards himself as merely contemptible in such a Presence, and abhors in dust

THE DIVINE INTERPRETATION 243

and ashes the thoughts which he had formerly expressed against God.

The divine discourse is divided into two parts by a brief dialogue of five verses, so that it may be regarded as two speeches. Some critics have regarded the second part as so inferior to the first that they have raised the question whether we have not here again an interpolation by another author. This suggestion, however, really rests upon no better foundation than the baseless supposition that a poet's work is usually so uniform in merit that he never falls much below the highest flights of his genius. The verdict of Dr Davidson on this point is not too emphatic when he says—" It may be said with certainty that the divine speeches belong to the original form of the book, and that they come from the hand of the author of the prologue." The conviction that this is so need not, however, in the least prevent us from recognising in the first part of the divine utterance out of the storm the most magnificent of all the many splendid examples of high peotic genius contained in the book.

Dr Driver says of it — " The first speech of Jehovah transcends all other descriptions of the wonders of the creation or the greatness of the Creator, which are to be found either in the Bible or elsewhere. Parts of II Isaiah (*e.g.* c. 40) approach it ; but they are conceived in a different strain, and, noble as they are, are less grand and impressive. The picturesque illustrations, the choice diction, the splendid imagery, the light and rapid movement of the verse, combine to produce a whole of incomparable brilliancy and force." Many other competent judges have like things to say of this wonderful speech ; and although it is generally admitted that the second part is not quite equal to the first, yet many consider that it is second to it alone, and that for grandeur of conception and majesty of expression this speech of Jehovah, taken as a whole, is without a parallel in all the literature of the world.

Job was now near the end of his great trial, and although he had passed through it successfully in the sense that he had not in the furnace of strange afflictions become an apostate, as Satan had predicted he would, yet he had so far given way to the strain and stress of the temptation to which he had been exposed that he had seriously erred both in thought and

THE DIVINE INTERPRETATION 245

speech regarding God, and had suffered his mind to take up something like a hostile attitude towards his Maker. Now the design of the first speech of Jehovah is to correct this rebellious element in the mind of Job, and to bring him back to a proper attitude of reverence and submission to God.

God proceeds to do this by a great display of His glory. But to imagine that by this display it is merely intended to impress Job with a bewildering mystery, or to oppress him by an overwhelming manifestation of power, would be to entirely misunderstand the aim of the divine speech. The speech is undoubtedly corrective, but it is none the less also truly restorative for that. It has it in a remarkable combination of majesty and gentleness. It is strongly coloured here and there with both reproach and rebuke; and sometimes the rebuke is so great that irony, and even stinging satire, are employed. Nevertheless, when we carefully consider the divine communication as a whole, we cannot fail to see that the tone of it is deeply gracious, and that the chief purpose of it is to win Job to a better state of mind, to bring him to a perfect reconciliation with God, and to establish his heart in a fuller and worthier trust in Him.

In the course of the debate with his friends Job had often been keenly pained by what he felt to be both the futility and the injustice of their arguments, and so he had frequently given passionate expression to his desire to get past these false advocates for God that he might come into direct contact with God Himself. Deep in the heart of Job there was a conviction of God's perfect justice, although he permitted himself to say to his friends, in answer to their misrepresentation of the truth, that the facts of Providence sometimes inclined him to another and a different conclusion. He therefore felt sure that if only he could get to close quarters with God He would not equivocate nor juggle with the facts as his friends did; and he was confident that he for his part could so order his cause before God as to convince Him of its justice, and to win from Him the admission that he was entirely in the right, and that his friends were completely in the wrong.

Now it was a true moral intuition that inspired Job with the faith that he would receive fairer and worthier treatment at the hands of God than

THE DIVINE INTERPRETATION 247

he had received from men ; but he had not truly foreseen what exactly the result of that treatment would be. He was now to have that opportunity of coming face to face with God for which he had so earnestly longed ; but the new revelation of God was to be so overpowering, and was to give him such a new revelation of himself in relation to such a Being, that it was to produce a very different impression upon him from that which he had expected, and was to make him cry out, like Isaiah in the temple, in the presence of God's overwhelming greatness and glory, that he was a man of unclean lips dwelling in the midst of a people of unclean lips. In other words, not self-justification but self-humiliation was to be the immediate result of his seeing the King, the Lord of Hosts. It was to be with him as with Newman's "Gerontius," according to the forecast of the angel :—

> "When then—if such thy lot—thou seest thy Judge,
> The sight of Him will kindle in thy heart
> All tender, gracious, reverential thoughts.
>   .   .   .   .   .   .
>   Thou wilt feel that thou hast sinned
> As never thou didst feel ; and wilt desire
> To slink away, and hide thee from His sight :
> And yet wilt have a longing aye to dwell
> Within the beauty of His countenance.

And these two pains, so counter and so keen—
The longing for Him when thou seest him not ;
The shame of self at thought of seeing Him,—
Will be thy veriest, sharpest purgatory."

We must not miss the central truth that at the heart of all this glorious self-revelation of God there dwells a redeeming tenderness. The end it has in view is not the crushing of Job into submission by reducing him to a state of terror in the presence of such dreadful majesty and power, but rather to open up to him new opportunities of realising at last what indeed is the true character of God, and also what are the deeper needs of his own life before him.

A new evidence of the high poetic genius of the author is seen in his manner of using the storm, the rising of which Elihu referred to in the latter part of his speech, as the medium of the divine manifestation. Job hears the voice of Jehovah in the voice of a storm great and prolonged, like his own great troubles. Probably there was in the mind of the poet the subtile intention of suggesting by this analogy the deep truth that it is when men are passing through the great trials of life that their hearts become more sensitive and their minds more open to

THE DIVINE INTERPRETATION 249

such divine communications as may become sources of spiritual inspiration to them in after years. Job was a good and upright man. And yet his behaviour under the terrible strain to which he had been subjected showed that he did not know God as he might and should have known Him; but now his great affliction had made him both more receptive and perceptive in regard to spiritual opportunities; and so he was now in a condition to benefit from the self-revelation of God about to be made to him in such a way as he never could have done at any previous period of his life.

The first part of the divine revelation is given to Job by a most magnificent description of the glory of God as it is exhibited in nature, first in the general phenomena of inanimate nature, and then in the region of animal life. The argument is addressed to his reason, but the appeal is for the response of his faith. Jehovah begins by charging Job with "darkening counsel" in the criticisms which he had passed upon His ways in Providence. The word "counsel" here is illuminative. It reminds Job that all things in Providence proceed according to a divine plan. What that plan was in relation to himself we know from the prologue; but we must remember that it was an essential part of Job's testing that he should not know it until after the testing was past.

What God claimed from Job was the exercise of a trust in Himself which went beyond his knowledge of the way by which God was leading him. It was not necessary for Job to have a full knowledge of God's plan of his life. It was enough if Job knew God Himself as One who was worthy to be trusted with the care and conduct of his life, amid whatever mystery and trouble, and One who would certainly find a way to fulfil His own good plan concerning His servant in the end. Job's attempt to reason out Providence had been a dismal failure, and had only succeeded in makng the mysteries of God's ways deeper and darker to his own mind.

It is always so: the world by its own wisdom never gets to a true knowledge of God; yet by that alone can peace and feeling come to the mind and heart of man; but such blessings can only come to the meek and quiet spirit of " them that believe." Jehovah seeks to bring salvation to Job by creating in him a worthy reverence for

THE DIVINE INTERPRETATION 251

and trust in Himself ; and this He seeks to do, not by justifying Himself to Job, nor by explaining the mysteries of Providence to him, which justification and explanation would probably have been beyond his grasp, but by making such a revelation of Himself to Job as was fitted to bring home to his heart and mind the fact that God was such an One as to be fully worthy of all the trust and reverence which He demanded, and which were required by the very nature of Job's own needs. Without faith it is always impossible to please God ; and without faith it is always equally impossible for man, in the deepest sense, to please himself.

Man has no deeper or more fundamental necessity in his nature, as the condition of his true peace and happiness than the exercise of a worthy faith in God. And how is he to rise to the possession of such a faith except by rising to such a knowledge of God as will be adequate to produce it ? Therefore God so reveals Himself to man as to enable him to attain to that end. This is the divine philosophy that determines the exact character of Jehovah's speech to Job out of the storm ; and a careful study of the speech as a whole will prove that this is so. For what we have in this great speech is not merely an incomparable description of the various wonders of nature that brings home to the human mind in a truly marvellous manner the power and wisdom of the Almighty; but we have here also a divine interpretation of nature which reveals the relation in which it stands, on the one hand to God as the expression of His character, and on the other hand to man, as a great medium by which he can grow in the knowledge of God and enter into fellowship with Him.

Now, of course, an exegetical commentary on this speech, which aims at explaining in detail the different words and phrases in it that present difficulties of interpretation, is a thing of great value; and this work has already been done by Dr Davidson in such a way as to leave very little indeed to be desired. But the transcendant beauty of these pictures of natural phenomena in earth and sea and sky, and of diverse kinds of living creatures, is such that it would be foolish to attempt to give anything like a detailed exposition of them here. They are to be read, and read again, and delighted in with wondering admiration; but the petals of those exquisite flowers of poetic genius and

THE DIVINE INTERPRETATION 253

spiritual inspiration are not to be rudely pulled about by common hands.

It is important, however, to note that the development of the thought proceeds along the line of a series of most impressive contrasts, in which the ignorance of Job is set over against the boundless knowledge of God; and the utter weakness of Job is contrasted with the tremendous power of God; and the fleeting nature of Job's days is dwarfed to nothingness by the eternity of the years of the Most High. These contrasts are brought out with the most overwhelming effect by the majestic manner in which God describes the wonders of His working in the different regions of nature. And we must not fail especially to note that all these tremendous powers that are so described are declared to be continually directed and controlled with high moral purpose, so that "from the wicked their light is withholden, and the high arm is broken."

The remarkable astronomical passage has been the subject of many curious comments. "Canst thou bind the cluster of the Pleiades, or loose the bands of Orion? Canst thou lead forth the Mazzaroth in their season? Or canst thou guide the Bear with her train? Knowest thou the ordinances of the heavens? Canst thou establish the dominion thereof in the earth?" Barnes remarks—"A somewhat curious use has been made of the reference to the stars in the book of Job, by an attempt to determine the time when he lived. Supposing the principal stars here mentioned to be those of Taurus and Scorpio, and that these were the cardinal constellations of spring and autumn in the time of Job, and calculating their position by the precession of the equinoxes, the time referred to in the book of Job was found to be 818 years after the deluge, or 184 years before the birth of Abraham. This calculation, made by Dr Brinkley of Dublin, and adopted by Dr Hales, had been made also in 1765 by M. Ducontant in Paris, with a result differing only in being forty-two years less." This reference, however, is merely curious, as, among other reasons, we have no means of knowing whether the heavenly bodies in the text are the same as those known to us under these names.

The thirty-sixth verse of chapter thirty-eight deserves special attention. "Who hath put wisdom in the inward parts? Or who hath given understanding to the mind?" Several scholars

THE DIVINE INTERPRETATION 255

have suggested that the passage should read—
" Who hath put wisdom in the cloud-masses ?
Or who hath given understanding to the metior ? "
If such a change be accepted, it certainly brings
the meaning of the verse into closer harmony
with the preceding verses. On the other hand,
if the common interpretation be retained, it
harmonises well with the verses which immediately follow, which suggests the limitations of the
human in contrast with the infinite powers of
the divine mind. The common meaning is also
very germane to the general argument of the
speech, which is to humble human pride in
the presence of God. This would be impressively
done by reminding Job that whatever powers
the human mind possessed were derived from
God as the Creator of man.

Of the wonderful descriptions of natural phenomena contained in this thirty-eighth chapter,
Dillmann has aptly said—" The attempt which
is here made to group together the overwhelming
marvels of nature, to employ them for the purpose
of producing an approximate impression of the
majesty of the Creator, though dependent upon
the childlike, but at the same time deeply poetical, view of nature prevalent in antiquity still,

retains not only its full poetical beauty, but also an imperishable religious worth. For though many of the phenomena here propounded as inexplicable are referred by modern science to their proximate causes, and comprehended under the general laws of nature, yet these laws themselves, by their unalterable stability and potent operation, only the more evoke our amazement, and will never cease to inspire the religious mind with adoring wonder at the infinite Power, Wisdom and Love, by which the individual laws and forces, and elements, are sustained and ruled."

At the thirty-ninth verse of the thirty-eighth chapter there is a change in the speech, and those magnificent word-pictures of natural phenomena are succeeded by another series equally as vivid and beautiful, and which are designed to show forth the manifold resources of the Creator as displayed in the animal kingdom. The creatures chosen as examples for this purpose are the lion, the raven, the wild goat, the wild ass, the wild ox, the ostrich, the horse, the hawk, and the eagle. These new pictures show a most intimate knowledge of the characteristics and habits of the different creatures described,

THE DIVINE INTERPRETATION 257

and these are all portrayed with marvellous poetic power. A careful examination of this second part of the speech, however, shows us that the end in view is exactly the same as that which ruled the first part of it, namely, to bring home to the mind of Job not only the power and wisdom of the Creator as seen in all the things and creatures which He has made, but also the ceaseless care which He exercises over all these, and the perfect control which He maintains over them all.

In the opening words of the fortieth chapter Jehovah addresses a direct challenge to Job which plainly indicates the chief purpose of the speech in relation to himself. " Moreover, the Lord answered Job, and said — Shall he that cavilleth contend with the Almighty? He that argueth with God, let him answer it." The aim of Jehovah, therefore, in thus addressing Job is to convince him that in cavilling and arguing with the Almighty he had been guilty of great folly and presumption. If a man takes up that attitude towards God, and persists in maintaining it, then he must be prepared to face the consequences. Job is reminded that, after all, the chief end of man is neither to criticise nor to interrogate his Maker, but to glorify Him. And in the very nature of the case a man can only do this by exercising a humble and loving trust in God. In the speech God has been showing Job that there is abundance of evidence in the works of God around him to assure him that God is worthy so to be trusted.

Now the reply of Job to this challenge of Jehovah shows what a tremendous impression has been produced upon him by the new revelation of God which he has just received. His reply presents a very striking contrast to the replies which he had given to his three friends. First of all we note that it is exceedingly brief. He had abundance of things to say in criticism of the ways of God to his friends, but when he is brought face to face with God Himself, he is struck dumb and, like the Apostle John in presence of Christ's risen glory, he is disposed to fall at God's feet as one dead. The second thing we note in Job's reply is that he has received a new revelation of his own insignificance in the presence of God. "Behold, I am of small account," he exclaims. As a very prosperous man his temptation had been to consider himself of much account, and he had shown this

THE DIVINE INTERPRETATION 259

repeatedly in the course of his arguments. Now in this new divine light he discovers that he had been thinking of himself as something when he was nothing, and had been so deceiving himself.

The third thing in Job's reply is a frank confession of the unanswerableness of Jehovah's arguments. "What shall I answer Thee?" he asks. "I lay mine hand upon my mouth." He had put his friends to silence by the ability of his arguments as opposed to theirs; but in presence of this new revelation of God Job had no arguments at all to offer; he felt that any arguments which he might offer were altogether out of place and even absurdly presumptuous in such a Presence. He was not only silenced, but he was humbled in the very dust. And so the last thing we note in Job's reply is the declaration of his firm determination to cease henceforth for ever from any attempt to criticise God or His ways. "Once I have spoken, and I will not answer; yea, twice, but I will proceed no further."

Jehovah now proceeds to the closing part of His discourse. He begins by declaring that He cannot be satisfied with the mere silence of

Job, and He demands some further answer. The idea seems to be that Job has not even yet either realised or confessed how seriously he has erred, and that only by such full recognition and confession of his sin could he either please God or obtain peace. Jehovah therefore brings a new charge against him and presses it upon him in such a way as is fitted to open his eyes more fully to his true position before God. This new charge is nothing less than this, that he has in his criticism of the moral government of God sought to justify himself at the expense of the reputation of the divine Ruler of all. So He demands of Job—" Wilt thou even disannul my judgment? Wilt thou condemn me that thou mayest be justified?"

The most serious thing about this charge is the motive which it suggests in Job, as if he actually considered his own character as more important than that of his Creator. In order to bring the full gravity of this charge home to the mind of Job God asks him whether he thinks that he is capable of taking His place in the government of the universe. What capacities, what knowledge, what power has Job to fit him to sustain the tremendous responsibilities involved

THE DIVINE INTERPRETATION 261

in such a position? There is a strong irony in the invitation which God gives to Job to show himself both worthy and able to take His place. " Hast thou an arm like God ? And canst thou thunder with a voice like Him ? Deck thyself now with excellency and dignity; and array thyself with honour and majesty; pour forth the overflowings of thine anger and look upon every one that is proud, and abase him. Look on every one that is proud, and bring him low; and tread down the wicked where they stand. Hide them in the dust together; bind their faces in the hidden place." Job is made to feel that so far from his being able to do any of these great things he is not even able to save himself from the just judgment of his own transgressions, and that his deliverance depends entirely upon the mercy of this same mighty God whom he had dared to criticise so freely.

Here follow detailed descriptions of two great creatures of the Nile, the Behemoth, or river ox, and the Leviathan, or crocodile. These are chosen as examples because of their extraordinary strength, and because they are so free from the fear and control of man that they are rather a terror to him. The argument is that if the creatures of God are so terrible to Job it is most foolish for him to think that he could stand before the revelation of the power of their Creator, with whom he has dared to contend. The Behemoth is described as "the chief of the ways of God." And of the Leviathan it is said—"None is so fierce that he dare stir him up"; and then follows immediately the question which plainly shows the divine intention in all this detailed description of these great creatures—"Who then is he that can stand before me? Who hath first given unto me, that I should repay him? Whatsoever is under the whole heaven is mine." Job is thus reminded that God alone is the fountain and source of all power, and that all these things to which He has been calling Job's attention are merely isolated examples of the workings of His omnipotence. How humble and reverent therefore should man be in presence of such a Being!

At the conclusion of this great speech of Jehovah there follows immediately the final reply of Job, which is full of self-abasement and penitence, and from which all traces of pride and self-justification have utterly vanished. He begins

THE DIVINE INTERPRETATION 263

by a humble acknowledgment of God's omnipotence. He is convinced of the utter futility of anyone attempting to resist God, and he is certain that no purpose of God can finally fail of its accomplishment. Then with chastened mind he meekly accepts the opening charge that God had made against him, namely, that he had been darkening counsel without knowledge. He takes this charge home to his heart as an established truth, and confesses that he has greatly erred through ignorance and presumption. " Therefore have I uttered that which I understood not, things too wonderful for me, which I knew not."

Then in a spirit of profound humility Job beseeches God to hear him, while he ventures to speak a few words in answer to the challenge which He had addressed to him. He quotes that challenge—" I will demand of thee, and declare thou unto me," as if he feels that his one plea for daring to answer God at all is that God had demanded an answer from him. His answer, which is in very few words, is that he has received a new revelation of God, which he finds to be a tremendous contrast to his old idea of God which he had while he was still bound with the bands of conventional and traditional religion. He felt that hitherto he had only known God as it were by hearsay, and by proxy; but now he knew God immediately and for himself. "I had heard of Thee by the hearing of the ear; but now mine eye seeth Thee."

The last word of Job's answer describes the effect which this new revelation of God had upon himself. He first says that it gave him a new view of himself, or, what is really the same thing, of the thoughts he had been thinking and the things he had been saying about God and His ways. And this new view of self led him to abhor that old self and the thoughts and speeches that grew out of it. And the other great service that this new revelation of God did for Job was that it gendered in him a new repentance, deeper and greater than he had ever known before, and which he felt operating with transforming and redeeming power through all his being, as the spring-tide works in nature, or as the daybreak works in the dark morning clouds. "I repent in dust and ashes," he cried. He felt that this new revelation of God had made him a new, a

THE DIVINE INTERPRETATION 265

humbler and a better man; and this was precisely what God desired and intended that it should do.

Now when we consider this speech of Jehovah as a whole, we are impressed by its undeniable incompleteness, and we are apt to feel somewhat disappointed in it, because we miss there some very important things which perhaps we not only expected it would contain, but which we are inclined to think it should contain. Reflection, however, will show that this feeling is due to our Christian consciousness, and to the great progress which revelation has made since the days in which this book was written. When we realise this we will recognise in these very omissions that trouble us, new proof of the genius, the modesty and the restraint of the sarced poet. We shall think with deeper wonder of those daring flights of speculative faith which he made in the speeches of Job. But we shall also admire his reserve and moderation when he comes to deal with the speech of the Almighty. He has shown, and that with great boldness, that religious thought has a right to claim and to exercise liberty; but now when God

Himself is the Speaker he has to show that this liberty must be restrained by certain limitations in order to protect it from degenerating into an unworthy licence. In this view there is nothing more remarkable about the divine speech than its omissions, the chief of which are these—

1. God does not blame Job, as the friends did, for being guilty of any special sin such as would account for his special sufferings. But, on the other hand, neither does God free Job from the charge of sin; on the contrary, He makes him feel that he has sinned in such a way that he is simply an object of the divine mercy.

2. God does not even begin to explain these deep mysteries of His Providence which had so profoundly perplexed Job. Throughout the whole speech He treats him in such a way as to remind him impressively that man is in no way responsible for the government of the universe, and that there are hidden things which belong to God alone.

3. God does not explicitly endorse Job's daring dream of a future life and of final vindication by a Redeemer; for the purpose of God in this

THE DIVINE INTERPRETATION 267

relation was not then explicable to man, and the time had not arrived for the full disclosure of the divine intention of salvation through a Redeemer, which was so far to transcend the dream of Job. Nevertheless, God does not in His speech discourage that daring hope; on the contrary, by implication He may be held to encourage it in His revelation of Himself as the just and righteous Ruler over all. And so that sublime dream of Job remains in some respects the most wonderful thing in the whole book.

4. God does not in His speech deal with the theory that human suffering is a gracious discipline which is intended to contribute in important ways towards the perfecting of human character. This is a very remarkable omission, not merely because its theory figured so conspicuously in the debate, but because it is so frequently referred to in other portions of the Old Testament.

5. God gives no judgment in the speech upon the interpretation which the friends had given of the moral government of the world. This is the more notable because this was one of the great subjects in the debate, and one

which is most nearly related to His own character. Divine judgment, however, is given against that interpretation in the epilogue.

6. God communicates to Job no special secret to meet his special need. Rather the new revelation of himself which He gives to Job is given along the lines of natural religion, and the media of its expression are such as are open to all men. Perhaps the lesson here intended is that in the storm of suffering the soul who endures it worthily attains to new powers of spiritual perception by which all things are seen as in a new light, a light that gives a new and wonderful interpretation even of the character of God Himself.

From these omissions we see how much was left for Christ to add in the interpretation of life's deepest questions. But it is equally interesting and instructive for us to note that the interpreattion of Christ agrees with that of the speech of Jehovah so far as it goes, although the new interpretation greatly transcends the old.

1. The whole ministry of Christ assumes that the supreme need of man is such a revelation of God as will awaken him to a new and true

THE DIVINE INTERPRETATION 269

sense of self as well as God, his own littleness and his own sinfulness before his Maker, that so he may attain to penitence and peace through a true faith in God. The great aim of Jehovah's speech may be admirably summed up in the words of Jeremiah—" Thus saith the Lord, let not the wise man glory in his wisdom, neither let the mighty man glory in his might, let not the rich man glory in his riches: but let him that glorieth glory in this, that he understandeth, and knoweth me, that I am the Lord which exercise loving kindness, judgment, and righteousness, in the earth; for in these things I delight, saith the Lord." Christ also taught in many forms that the true knowledge of God is the supreme glory of the human soul. He said: "This is life eternal, that they should know Thee the only true God, and Him whom Thou didst send, even Jesus Christ."

2. Another great characteristic of Jehovah's speech to Job is that it teaches emphatically that men may so know God through His works as to be led not only to apprehend His power and wisdom, but also to trust in His loving care. This is a truth which Christ also taught

in His own incomparable way. "Behold the birds of the heaven, that they sow not, neither do they reap, nor gather into barns ; and your heavenly Father feedeth them. Are not ye of much more value than they ? " "Consider the lilies of the field, how they grow ; they toil not, neither no they spin : yet I sayun to you, that even Solomon in all his glory was not arrayed like one of these. But if God doth so clothe the grass of the field, which to-day is, and to-morrow is cast into the oven, shall He not much more clothe you, O ye of little faith ? "

3. But the revelation which Jesus Christ gave of God in His own divinely human life immeasurably transcended all that could ever have been known of God through nature. God was in Christ reconciling the world unto Himself. He revealed Himself in the human life of Christ as He never could reveal Himself elsewhere ; so that Christ, and Christ alone, could say—" He that hath seen me hath seen the Father."

4. By God's way of dealing with Job we see how a *good* man can be reconciled to God. But the problem which the ministry of Christ

THE DIVINE INTERPRETATION 271

solves is a far deeper one, and the revelation which He gives of the divine heart is far more wonderful. "The Son of Man came to seek and to save that which was *lost.*" Christ justifies the creation of the worst of men by providing a salvation which is adequate to the deepest need even of the chief of sinners. He is not merely the pattern of the good, but He is also the Saviour of the bad, and even to the uttermost.

5. Christ gave a new and higher interpretation of human pain than anything we have in the book of Job. He said of the man born blind—"Neither did this man sin, nor his parents: but that the works of God should be made manifest to him." There are sufferers who are God's living object-lessons to their brethren, to teach them lessons that they could learn no otherwise. "Prosperity," said Bacon, "is the blessing of the Old Testament; adversity that of the new Testament, which is the mark of God's more especial favour. Yet even in the Old Testament, if you listen to David's harp, you shall hear as many hearse-like airs as carols; and the pencil of the Holy Ghost has laboured more in describing the afflictions of Job than the felicities of Solomon."

Certainly Christ has given a new interpretation to the mystery of human pain, and He has done this not only by His teaching but especially by His life, and supremely by His death. He has shown us how God is able to fulfil the wonderful word of the old Hebrew prophet and to turn not only the shadow of pain but even the shadow of death into the morning.

6. Finally, Christ not only confirmed the daring dream of Job concerning a future life and man's relation to God therein; but He gave a revelation of the future which far surpassed Job's dream. He brought life and immortality to light. He made His followers see that the most inexplicable suffering can be transformed in resurrection light. He made the thought of heaven a dear familiar thing to all believing hearts as the Father's House, the eternal Home of all who love God and sincerely seek the good. He related this life to that future life in such deep and fundamental ways that men of faith were able even to glory in tribulations in order that the power of Christ might rest upon them; so that they ceased to think of the grave as the grim portal to a shadowy Sheol, but knew

THE DIVINE INTERPRETATION 273

it as the gateway of unshdaowed light and of glorious reward.

Christ called upon his followers to rejoice and be exceeding glad, even in the midst of the most terrible persecution, because great was their reward in heaven; and they, in the power of that great new hope with which He had inspired them, responded to that call, and were able to say, even in such circumstances as these—" Our light affliction, which is but for a moment, worketh for us more and more exceedingly an eternal weight of glory; while we look not at the things which are seen, but at the things which are not seen; for the things which are seen are temporal; but the things which are not seen are eternal. For we know that if the earthly house of our tabernacle be dissolved, we have a building from God, a house not made with hands eternal in the heavens."

Thus may we see how great a difference the coming of Christ has made; and thus may we feel how imperfectly Job could know God when He spoke to him as a Voice out of the storm in comparison with the way in which we are privileged to know Him, when He speaks to us

s

with the human lips of His incarnate Son, and when we behold and see, not the terror of His power working in dreadful splendours in the black breast of the thunder-cloud, but " the light of the knowledge of the glory of God in the face of Jesus Christ."

CHAPTER XI

THE EPILOGUE

WE come now in conclusion to consider the epilogue of this great book. This, like the prologue, is written in simple prose, and its style forms a striking contrast to that employed in the main body of the work, which, as we have seen, is amazingly rich in most sublime examples of high poetic genius.

Some critics regard the epilogue as a surprise, and think it so unnecessary that they make it a new ground for raising further questions about the integrity of the book. This is so remarkable a view to take of the epilogue that only something like a passion for reducing the book to as many fragments as possible could account for any student of the work entertaining it at all. For it seems to be undeniable that there is no part of the book more imperatively required for its completeness, and for the purpose of establishing the chief points for which the author has been contending all along, than this concluding part of the work.

It is plain that without the epilogue a false impression could hardly fail to be left upon the mind of the reader. If the last word of the book were Job's humble confession that he repented in dust and ashes, then the suffering servant of Jehovah would seem to be left crushed and defeated. The reader would be left to suppose that he had failed under the trial to which he had been subjected, and that the three friends who had criticised him so severely were right in their contentions after all.

Moreover, without the epilogue the teaching of the book would be undoubtedly fatalistic in its tendency. It would give the impression that man is the subject of an almighty and inscrutable power before whose decrees he must bow with stoical resignation, and without any assurance of ultimate vindication or reward. A divine verdict was therefore absolutely needed to give an authoritative decision upon the respective parts played by Job and his friends unless the book was to fail

THE EPILOGUE

in regard to one of the chief purposes for which it was written. Job had confidently predicted that such a verdict would be given, and he had tried to lead his friends to a juster and more sympathetic treatment of the case by awakening within them an apprehension of what that verdict was bound to be as proceeding from a just God. Without it therefore the work of the author would have been left in a singularly imperfect condition; and we have every reason to be well assured that the epilogue formed an essential part of the original book.

The epilogue begins with an intimation of the divine anger against the three friends. " And it was so that after the Lord had spoken these words unto Job, the Lord said to Eliphaz the Temanite, My wrath is kindled against thee and against thy two friends: for ye have not spoken of me the thing that is right, as my servant Job hath." The verdict is addressed to Eliphaz probably because he was the eldest of the three friends, and he was the first and chief speaker. But the remarkable thing about the divine verdict is the reason that is given for the divine anger. It is not because of the way in which the friends have spoken about Job, but the way in which they have spoken about God.

This is in every way highly significant. In the first place it is precisely the opposite of what we might have expected; for whereas Job, as Jehovah had just been showing in his address to him, had said many things which could not be justified against God, the friends, on their part, had never, any of them, said anything which was not what they considered most favourable to God; and, on the other hand, they had not hesitated to say many severe and even cruel things against Job, and these things they had been led to say chiefly because Job was so impiously bold, as they thought, in speaking against God.

We might therefore have naturally expected that as Jehovah had reproved Job for the way in which he had spoken against Himself, so now He would reprove the friends for the way in which they had spoken against Job. But the ground of God's anger against the friends is not what they had said about Job, but that they had not spoken of Himself the thing that that was right. Here we are reminded once

THE EPILOGUE

more of the high reverence which the author has for God, and our minds are brought back to the origin of the whole trial as it was presented to us in the prologue. It is often suggested in the book that the reputation of man is of small account in comparison with the reputation of God, but this is nowhere more strikingly done than here.

This statement, "Ye have not spoken of me the thing that is right, as my servant Job hath," is repeated to indicate the author's estimate of its peculiar importance. The reference is to the theory of God's Providence which had been the chief subject of discussion between Job and his friends. They had not spoken that which was right about God, because in their determination to be the champions of God only in the line of championing their own theory of his moral government they had equivocated with inconvenient facts, and they had sometimes spoken as partisans of God, so that they might whitewash the providence of God. Job on the other hand, although he had been over-bold in his criticisms, and had been reproved for this by God, had nevertheless always been sincere, and had sought to dealt honestly with the hard facts of life in such a way as to reach the actual truth, whether it might support, or condemn his previous cherished ideas. Here, therefore, the author emphatically claims that, in the sight of God, the way of Job is right, and the way of the friends is wrong.

The next element in the divine verdict is the declaration of the need of atonement and intercession for the three friends, and the command that they should seek Job to perform this important function on their behalf. In the prologue Job is introduced to us as the high priest of his own family: in the sequel he is called upon to act the same part on behalf of his critics and accusers. It is to be noted that there is no mention of any official priesthood in the book; and this is another evidence of the great antiquity, not indeed of the book as it now stands, but of the period in which Job lived, pointing to a very primitive and patriarchal mode of life. The friends had undertaken to be the expositors of the ways of God to Job; but they are now required to seek him as

THE EPILOGUE

their priest and mediator between God and themselves. They are commanded to take with them seven bullocks and seven rams as an offering for sacrifice, the number seven indicating completeness.

Then nothing could be more emphatic and complete, as a vindication of Job as opposed to the friends in regard to those great matters about which they had so strenuously contended, than what follows—"And my servant Job shall pray for you; for him will I accept, that I deal not with you after your folly." Now the very things which these three men had prided themselves about in all their discussions with Job were their wisdom and their piety—their acceptableness with God. They had reasoned themselves into the belief that Job was a specially wicked man; and they had done their best to convince him that for no other reason could he be subjected, in the providence of a just God, to the calamities and sufferings which he was enduring. They had been very confident that this argument was as wise as it was pious. In urging it upon Job's acceptance they had complacently regarded themselves as the servants of Jehovah; and when he rejected it with indignation they had denounced his words as those of a vain wind-bag, whose mind was ruled by the spirit of folly, and whose heart was full of such impiety as could not fail to attract the righteous judgment of God.

But now by the divine verdict all this human judgment is entirely reversed. They are shown to be the men of folly and Job the man of true wisdom: they are condemned as men lacking in genuine piety, and Job is found to be the one man among them who has the spirit of a true worshipper: they are rejected as men who had offered to God a service that did Him real dishonour, but Job is accepted as a man who had proved himself to be God's true servant, by holding fast to the truth against all appearances, and by serving Him with such a clear honesty and such a pure motive as did honour to himself as well as to God. And the irony of the situation found its climax in this, that Job became the divinely appointed means of delivering his would-be reformers from the judgment which they deserved.

THE EPILOGUE

Thus we see that the divine command to the three friends involved the most extreme humiliation for them. Nevertheless they found grace to obey it, and so they obtained pardon and reconciliation; for "the Lord accepted Job," and blessed them for Job's sake, and through Job's intercession, according to His promise.

But all this is only the first stage of the divine vindication of Job; and there follow immediately two things which complete his triumph, namely, his perfect deliverance from all his pains and troubles, and his restoration to far more than all his former greatness and prosperity.

There is something beautifully suggestive in the words by which this second stage of Job's vindication is introduced—"And the Lord turned the captivity of Job, when he prayed for his friends." It would doubtless be too much to say that Job's deliverance and restoration were conditional upon his praying for his friends; but it is not overstating the truth to say that the possession of the spirit that enabled him so to pray for his friends alone made his deliverance and restoration possible.

There is no mention of any divine command

to Job that he should accede to the request of his former accusers to pray for them. Nor is there any intimation that the friends made known to Job the fact that they came with their request by divine command. Job may have been as ignorant of this as he was of the accusations of Satan which led to his great trial. At any rate Job immediately rose to the full height of the great opportunity which the three friends thus presented to him; and we can hardly doubt that the author meant to indicate by this a great moral victory on the part of Job, suggesting the spiritual progress which he had made by means of all the discipline through which he had passed.

When we consider the record of Job's restoration we are reminded once more that in this book we are not dealing with ordinary history as we understand it. There is a manifest ideality in the blessings bestowed upon him. It is not merely said in a general way that his possessions were doubled; but the minute details of this doubling process are given. The seven hundred sheep of the prologue become fourteen hundred; the three thousand camels are now exactly six thousand; the five hundred yoke of oxen become a thousand; and the five hundred she-asses are also raised to exactly twice that number. His new children also exactly replace those that perished, not only in regard to number but even in regard to sex, there being seven sons and three daughters.

No further mention is made of Job's wife, who played so poor a part in the drama, and of whom we last heard in Job's second reply to Bildad, when he said—"My breath is strange to my wife." We are therefore left to suppose that these new children are probably the fruit of a second marriage. Of Job's kindred, however, we read—"Then came there unto him all his brethren, and all his sisters, and all they that had been his acquaintance before, and did eat bread with him in his house: and they bemoaned him, and comforted him concerning all the evil that the Lord had brought upon him." We last hear of these friends also in Job's second reply to Bildad, when he says—"He hath put my brethren far from me, and mine acquaintance are wholly estranged from me. My kinsfolk have failed, and my familiar friends have forgotten me."

We might have supposed that in his restored

prosperity Job would be well content to be rid of such fair-weather friends, and would at any rate find no special joy in their reappearance when their chance of giving was gone and their opportunity to receive had returned. But here again we see the ideality of the narrative. We see another indication of the same thing in the statement that every man who came to visit Job in his new state brought for him a piece of money, and every one also a ring of gold.

The statement that, "After this Job lived an hundred and forty years, and saw his sons, and his sons' sons, even four generations," is evidently made as giving additional proof of the divine favour and blessing. But besides this it is also of interest as throwing some light upon the question as to the time in which Job lived. The translators of the Septuagint render this passage thus—"And Job lived after this affliction an hundred and seventy years: so that all the years that he lived were two hundred and forty." What ground they had for assuming that Job was seventy years old when his troubles began, or on what authority they added thirty years to those assigned to him in the Hebrew text after his troubles were past, we have no means of ascertaining. Remembering, however, that he belonged to the patriarchal period, and that he was the father of ten children at the beginning of the story it seems not unreasonable to suppose that he was then about seventy years old.

It is fair to suppose also that the age of Job is given not as being in any sense miraculous, but as indicating something like the extreme limit of human life at that period of the world's history. And when in additions to these considerations we remember that Nahor lived two hundred and forty-eight years, Terah two hundred and five years, Abraham one hundred and seventy-five years, and Isaac one hundred and eighty years, we have reasonable data for fairly approximating the time at which Job lived. The concluding statement of the Septuagint— "And it is written that he will rise again with those whom the Lord will raise up"— may safely be regarded as having nothing to do with the original text, but as the addition of some scribe of a long subsequent time.

We may regard the epilogue as a whole as a picture of poetic justice; but we shall fail to appreciate its deepest significance unless we perceive it to be much more than this. We can only understand its true meaning if we recognise it as an organic part of the book and see how essentially it is related to the trial of Job, and to the deep moral questions discussed in connection with it. It is not by isolating the different parts of the book from each other, but rather by seeing their true relation to each other, that we shall apprehend its real greatness and put it to its highest uses. It may therefore be of some service, if, in concluding these studies, I endeavour to sum up briefly what I conceive to be the principal teaching of the book, considered as a whole.

1. A fundamental part of the teaching of the book is that the life of man is so related to unseen Powers, both good and evil, that it is conditioned by that relation in ways that are beyond his knowledge. This is a belief which has had a very general hold upon the minds of men in all lands, and in all ages, and it has found various modes of expressing itself in the different religions of the world. It is out of this relation of man to the unseen powers that the whole trial of Job springs, as we see in the prologue of the book. The attack of Satan is really an attack upon God,

THE EPILOGUE

although it is made upon God indirectly through His creature man. It is the honour of God that is challenged when the motive of His creature's service is brought in question by the Satanic sneer—" Doth Job serve God for naught ? " But there is no suggestion of anything that deserves to be called Dualism in the book. Jehovah is not only just and gracious, but He is also almighty and supreme, and the Satan can only trouble man so far as he obtains permission from God to do so. But the origin of his troubles is unknown to Job.

2. Another intention of the author seems to have been to teach the insufficiency of human reason and the need of divine revelation for the true explanation of the deeper things in human experience. All competent judges admit that there is a most brilliant display of the loftiest powers of the human mind in the great debate between Job and his friends. But the author shows that all that can be said, on the one side and on the other, is utterly inadequate to meet and satisfy the great deep needs of the heart and of the mind in a case like that of Job. He suggests that much can be learned from the dim revelation which God makes of Himself in nature,

T

but he plainly indicates that something much more definite and intimate is needed, some personal communication, some Voice out of the storm, and in the highest flights of his spiritual genius he even dares to hope for a Daysman-Redeemer who shall so combine the human and the divine as to be the perfect interpreter and mediator between them.

3. Another thing which this ancient Hebrew poet undoubtedly meant to teach was the serious dangers of a merely conventional and traditional religion. All the three friends of Job, and even Elihu also, are meant to be impressive examples of this, and in their successive speeches against Job the author shows us with cumulative effect all the hardness, and the narrowness, and the shallowness, all the uncharity, and the cruelty, and the injustice that may creep into the hearts of both good and able men, when they have handed themselves over as the bond slaves of a merely traditional religion. He shows how it steels the heart, not only against the claims of friendship, but even against the ordinary compassions of humanity, and how it even leads men to play fast and loose with

THE EPILOGUE 291

the truth in order that they may support their traditional dogmatic theology.

4. Then over against this false orthodoxy, which did not hesitate even to lie for God, and to speak deceitfully for Him, it was evidently the intention of the author of this book to vindicate the liberty of religious thought. This is done with extraordinary power in the successive speeches of Job. The author indicates that this liberty has definite and necessary limitations, and not only in the speeches of Jehovah, but also in the repentance of Job, he clearly admits that the sufferer has here and there seriously trespassed these limits. Yet no student of the book can fail to be convinced that this vindication of the liberty of religious thought was one of the chief purposes for which it was written. The author felt that all the extreme boldness of the thought and language of Job was needed to shake the orthodox cowardice, represented in the three friends, out of its unmeasured self-complacency.

5. Another unquestionable intention of the inspired author was to give a new interpretation of the relation between sin and human suffering. The unfolding of this interpretation

occupies a large portion of the book and constitutes one of the principal elements in its teaching. The old view of the relation between sin and suffering was that just as prosperity was the divine reward of virtue, so suffering was the penal consequence of sin. This view is fully represented in the speeches of the friends. The author was profoundly convinced that this view was hopelessly opposed to the undeniable facts of life.

In his new interpretation of the relation between sin and suffering he does not teach that suffering is never penal, but only that it is not always so. He teaches also that human suffering is often inflicted as a gracious corrective to restore men who were wandering from the path of virtue, and that it is sometimes imposed as a preventive to save men from sins which they have not yet committed, but into which they have a tendency to fall. But above all, the author unfolds his strikingly original idea that men are sometimes called to suffer as the champions of God, not for any sin which they have done, or are likely to do, but that they may make a new revelation of human love for and trust in God, revealing in their

THE EPILOGUE 293

suffering, as they could not otherwise, how they love God, not merely for what He gives, but for what He is, and how they can trust in Him, not only beyond their understanding, but against all appearances. The author clearly shows that he had this purpose in his mind at the very beginning of the work, and he carries it out with great originality and power.

6. Another important and cognate teaching purpose of the book is to set forth what the attitude of a good man should be when he is confronted with the inexplicable mysteries of Providence. That attitude, the author shows, should be one of frank and honest courage, and yet there should always be associated with that courage a deep and reverent humility. He indicates that both Job and his friends erred here, they because they were destitute of the honest courage, and he because amid the terrible pressure of his sufferings he did not maintain that reverent humility which is always due from man in relation to God. Again and again in the progress of the debate the author shows how great and noble a part faith has to play in this connection, and the splendid and illuminative bursts of faith to

294 AFFLICTIONS OF THE RIGHTEOUS

which Job rises form an impressive contrast to the feeble and mechanical confidence of the friends in their discredited orthodoxy, which is not far removed from a credulous superstition. It is by this contrast that the author seeks to show how, in the words of Robert Browning:

> " While when the scene of life shall shift,
> And the gay heart he taught to ache,
> As sorrows and privations take
> The place of joy,—the thing that seems
> Mere misery, under human schemes,
> Becomes, regarded by the light
> Of love, as very near, or quite
> As good a gift as joy before."

This is the lesson which is perfectly taught by the experience of Paul in connection with his " thorn in the flesh," whatever that was, which experience led him to this remarkable conclusion—" Most gladly, therefore, will I rather glory in my weaknesses, that the strength of Christ may rest upon me."

7. Finally, I do not think it can be doubted that the author of this book intended to teach the necessity of a divine revision of human judgments upon human conduct, and the certainty of the ultimate vindication of a good

THE EPILOGUE

man's life. He does this by showing us how unfair, and even cruel, were the judgments which his friends passed upon Job, although these could be supported with a certain measure of plausibility in relation to the accepted doctrines of the time. He shows us, however, that these judgments were based upon ignorance of certain high realities of the unseen world revealed to us in the prologue, and also upon a radical misconception of the providence of God. Therefore that human judgment needs to be reversed, and is reversed, by the divine judgment pronounced in the epilogue.

Some critics have said that this being so, the closing scene, like the opening one, should have been laid, not on earth, but in heaven. But we have already seen that the sacred poet was limited in this connection by the conditions of the time, and that because revelation had then reached only an early stage, it was impossible for him to use the future life and heaven in ways that are familiar to our Christian consciousness, but which were unknown to him. The wonder rather is that this ancient Hebrew poet should have been able by his piercing spiritual perception to anticipate, in the marvellous manner he does, revelations which were being kept in store for an age then in the far distant future.

In the epilogue he pictures in the best way open to him the ultimate divine vindication of the good man's life. And the Apostle of Christ still thinks of that ancient picture as being worthy of the earnest attention of Christian men and women, as a source of rich comfort, and as a means of enabling them to bear their trials more worthily. " Ye have heard," says James, " of the patience of Job, and have seen the end of the Lord, how that the Lord is full of pity, and merciful." Often it is only "the end of the Lord " which truly and fully interprets His beginning. And perhaps the chief thing which this great teacher of the ancient past meant to teach by the experience of Job was just the same thing which another great modern teacher seeks to teach anew in his song of Rabbi Ben Ezra, but with an added confidence and clearness, which the new light fully justifies—

" Grow old along with me !
The best is yet to be,
The last of life, for which the first was made :

THE EPILOGUE

Our times are in His hand
Who saith, 'A whole I planned,
Youth shows but half; trust God : see all, nor be afraid !
 . . . .
     Praise be Thine !
  I see the whole design,
I, who saw power, see now love perfect too :
  Perfect I call Thy plan :
  Thanks that I am a man !
Maker, remake, complete,—I trust what Thou shalt do."

www.ingramcontent.com/pod-product-compliance
Lightning Source LLC
Chambersburg PA
CBHW022054230426
43672CB00008B/1173